A DIFFERENT COUNTRY
RUSSIA'S ECONOMIC RESURGENCE

LÚCIO VINHAS DE SOUZA

CENTRE FOR EUROPEAN POLICY STUDIES
BRUSSELS

The Centre for European Policy Studies (CEPS) is an independent policy research institute based in Brussels. Its mission is to produce sound analytical research leading to constructive solutions to the challenges facing Europe today. CEPS Paperbacks present analysis and views by leading experts on important questions in the arena of European public policy, written in a style geared to an informed but generalist readership.

The author, Lúcio Vinhas de Souza, is the official responsible for Russia at the Directorate-General for Economic and Financial Affairs of the European Commission. The views expressed in this report are those of the author writing in a personal capacity and do not necessarily reflect those of CEPS, the European Commission or any other institution with which he is associated.

Cover photo: Construction site in Moscow, September 2007

ISBN 13: 978-92-9079-767-8
© Copyright 2008, Centre for European Policy Studies.

Centre for European Policy Studies
Place du Congrès 1, B-1000 Brussels
Tel: 32 (0) 2 229.39.11 Fax: 32 (0) 2 219.41.51
e-mail: info@ceps.eu
Internet: http://www.ceps.eu

CONTENTS

List of Figures

List of Tables

List of Boxes

Я к вам пишу – чего же боле?

Что я могу еще сказать?

А.С. Пушкин

"I write to you – what more can I do?
What else can I say?"

From *Evgeny Onegin* by Alexsandr Pushkin

EXECUTIVE SUMMARY

Russia is now once again one of the ten largest economies in the world (representing around 80% of Germany's GDP in purchasing power parity in 2007). Additionally, Russia is the third largest trade partner of the EU, the fourth largest trade partner of the eurozone and an essential energy supplier to the EU. This recovery makes Russia an economic – and political – actor that cannot be ignored, and arguably also a *different country.*[1]

This book describes the country's evolving policy framework and macroeconomic performance, from the difficult days of the 'transition recession' and the 1998 crisis to the sustained and robust growth since 1999, which is only partially related to the energy price cycle. It considers several different components of the improved Russian macro and microeconomic frameworks. The study also looks at some of the remaining reform priorities and provides policy recommendations.

Chapter 1 of this book describes the substantial changes observed in Russia since the end of the USSR. It charts the initial period of economic and social dislocation following the collapse of the Soviet Union and the introduction of market economy institutions, to the apparent stabilisation of the mid-1990s and the subsequent crisis of 1998. It also traces the

---

[1] This description (and the title of this book) is of course a play on the words contained in the titles of the papers by Shleifer & Treisman (2005), "A Normal Country: Russia after Communism" and Rosefielde (2005), "Russia: An Abnormal Country", which engage in that traditional Western discussion of how 'normal' Russia is.

resumption of growth from 1999 onwards, generated by the accumulated effects of economic and structural reforms and high energy prices. Chapter 1 also shows that Russia's macroeconomic performance has actually not been any less than that of truly similar countries, either before or after 1998. The length and intensity of its transitional recession were related to the later start of reforms in the CIS countries, the depth of distortions accumulated by three generations of a centrally planned economy and the lack of a truly binding external anchor. The situation was further aggravated by the break-up of the Soviet Union.

Chapter 2 looks at some of the remaining reform challenges for the fiscal and monetary systems, foreign direct investment, competitiveness, the energy sector, social development and state reform. It also argues that in terms of structural reform, when benchmarked against broadly similar economies – either other CIS countries or the other emerging giants of the BRICs (Brazil, Russia, India and China) – Russia's performance is impressive. All the fundamental structures of a market economy have been established and the macroeconomic framework is much more robust than it was in the mid-1990s. Additionally, despite the perception conveyed by some analyses, structural reform – albeit slower in certain areas – has not stopped. That is not to say that a substantial, unfinished reform agenda does not remain: it does, and it includes some macro components, but mostly microeconomic and structural ones. Chapter 2 therefore also looks at this unfinished reform agenda. In terms of the macro challenges, how to cope with the reduction and eventual disappearance of the current account surplus is likely to be the most important matter for medium-term policy. This change will imply a need for continued positive net capital inflows, and the related need for a reliable investment climate, which is linked to the reform of the Russian state institutions and policies. Continued support for the reform of the wider apparatus of the Russian state and for the international *fora* that enable the sharing of international best practice with the Russian government are a part of this. The full use of external anchors for reform (the G8, WTO accession, OECD membership plus the extensive network of agreements and *fora* between the EU and Russia – the future EU–Russia framework agreement and eventual EU–Russia deep free trade agreement and the EU–Russia Sectoral Dialogues) is a feasible, necessary and important part of this strategy.

Chapter 3 concludes the book with a summary of the previous chapters and their recommendations.

ACKNOWLEDGEMENTS

T he essays brought together in this book were originally prepared as individual internal background notes and literature reviews within the European Commission. Several of those original notes and papers were written in collaboration with Andreas Papadopoulos and José Leandro from the Directorate-General for Economic and Financial Affairs (DG ECFIN), for which this author is grateful.

Given their original purpose, these background briefs, notes and papers were not initially planned as a single work, but rather as separate essays addressing subjects of perceived importance concerning Russia in the economic area. This explanation accounts for the absence of chapters on politics, trade and the institutional framework for relations between the EU and Russia. Their unifying theme is Russia's economic trajectory since the early 1990s and the outstanding challenges for growth sustainability in that country.

I would also like to thank CEPS Director Daniel Gros, several colleagues at various Directorates-General of the European Commission and an anonymous referee for their comments on an earlier version of this work. I would also like to thank Anne Harrington and Kathleen King at CEPS for the wonderful (and patient) editing work. The views expressed here are mine and do not necessarily reflect the official views of the European Commission. The usual disclaimers apply.

Lúcio Vinhas de Souza
April 2008, Brussels

1. RUSSIA'S ECONOMIC PERFORMANCE: THE 1991-2008 'TRANSITIONS'

This chapter presents the reform process in Russia during the 1990s, from Gorbachev to Yeltsin. It also discusses the associated macroeconomic performance of the 'newly independent' Russia, from the early 1990s until the latter part of the 2000s.

1.1 Economic reform[2] in Russia during the early 1990s

1.1.1 Gorbachev and incidental reforms

Formally, the end of the Union of Socialist Soviet Republics (USSR or Soviet Union) took place in early December 1991, but actually, the collapse of the Soviet Union and of the associated planned economic system did not occur at a single moment in time. Effectively, it had already begun with the economic slowdown (Ofer, 1987) observed during the long Brezhnev government (1964–82), and it was arguably accelerated by the partial economic liberalisation reforms undertaken during the Gorbachev government (1985-91).

---

[2] A transition process from central planning to a market-based economy has to fulfil two fundamental and interdependent goals, macroeconomic stabilisation and microeconomic/structural reform (see Vinhas de Souza, 2003), which must occur in parallel with the integration of an autarky into the rest of the world economy. The former entails implementing consistent, stability-oriented fiscal and monetary policies, while the latter requires establishing all the frameworks (legal and institutional) necessary for a market economy to operate efficiently (including the legalisation of private property and price liberalisation).

Economic reform had also started *before* the 1991 break-up of the Soviet Union,[3] and the path and limits of this economic reform process in the country cannot be understood separately from the *political constraints* faced by the Soviet/Russian leadership. The partial economic liberalisation under President Mikhail Gorbachev[4] (the six years of the so-called 'perestroika'[5] period) ultimately failed, but brought a foretaste of things to come (Mau & Starodubrovskaya, 2001). Central planning was restricted[6] and later limited incentives for the development of private enterprises were introduced through the legalisation of small cooperatives, joint ventures with state enterprises and local councils, and self-employment.[7]

---

[3] The *official* end of the Soviet Union happened on 8 December 1991, when Russian President Boris Yeltsin met with the Presidents of Ukraine and Belarus, Leonid Kravchuk and Stanislau Shushkevich, at the Belovezhskaya Pushcha Natural Reserve in Belarus. There the three presidents announced the dissolution of the Soviet Union and the establishment of a (voluntary) Commonwealth of Independent States (CIS) in its place. Mr Yeltsin's decision to call this meeting was kept secret from the incumbent Soviet Union President Mikhail Gorbachev.

[4] Mikhail Sergeyevich Gorbachev was born in 1931 in the village of Privolnoya in the Caucasus. He ascended from Regional Party Leader to the Politburo within the Communist Party under the protection of Yuri Andropov, the (reformist) KGB head who was briefly Secretary General of the Communist Party of the Soviet Union (i.e. president of the USSR) for 15 months between 1982 and 1984.

[5] Perestroika means restructuring. This economic reform component was supposed to be developed in tandem with another component involving political reform, more specifically 'glasnost' [openness].

[6] The restriction was affected through the June 1987 Law of State Enterprise. With this law, central planning was replaced by a 'state orders system', covering some of the manufacturing industries and enabling them to sell a share of their production in the 'free market'. This law also allowed the closure of loss-making enterprises. In practical terms, this reform had limited effectiveness, as the pricing and supply structures that enterprises dealt with remained unchanged.

[7] The legalisation occurred through the May 1988 Law on Cooperatives. Many of the companies formed under this law engaged in exports, as they were able to access commodities at controlled prices and sell them at world market prices with significant profits. The 1989 Law on Leasing also enabled employees to lease state enterprises with a right to a subsequent full buy-out. These laws are the true origin of the Russian oligarch class that was to reach its maturity with the privatisation programme of the 1990s.

These were important but piecemeal reforms. Moreover, a supporting policy mix was absent: fiscal and monetary latitude contributed to an increase of the pre-existing monetary overhang.[8] Meanwhile, the external position of the Soviet Union had become relatively vulnerable in the late 1980s, owing to cyclically low oil prices (which led to the accumulation of external debt, partially to support a surge in the imports of consumer goods).

The explanation for this limited and inconsistent set of reforms lies in the diminishing support President Gorbachev encountered within the dominant political force in the USSR at the time, the bureaucratic and state apparatus of the Communist Party (Neville, 2003). Furthermore, this was not the first time that a partial reform of the centrally planned economy had failed in the Soviet Union: previous attempts include the 1921–29 New Economic Policy and the 1965–68 abortive reform of the incentives system (Mau & Starodubrovskaya, 2001).

Of course, one of the main goals of perestroika (and glasnost) was the weakening of the Communist Party itself, but another contradiction within the reform process constrained the achievement of this goal – Mr Gorbachev's own personal loyalties. He seemingly never intended fully to replace either the centrally planned economy or the Soviet Union (Mau & Starodubrovskaya, 2001; Kotz & Weir, 2007). This ambiguity on the part of the leader of the initial reform process also substantially explains its ultimate failure.

The perestroika inconsistencies were only overcome by the appearance of a new political force, in the form of Boris Yeltsin, the first President of the newly 'independent' Russian Federation.[9]

---

[8] Traditionally, in centrally planned economies, *markets fail to clear*, i.e. supply and demand do not balance. In a market economy, the adjustment would be through prices in such a situation. As prices were controlled in the Soviet economies, *unused* monetary balances that could not be converted to goods or services – as these were not available – would be accumulated by households and firms. The liberalisation of prices and external trade, besides the macro balance and allocative micro-efficiency issues involved, aimed to eliminate some of this surplus.

[9] Boris Nikolayevich Yeltsin was born in 1931 in the Sverdlovsk *oblast*. A popular 'mayor' of Moscow (formally the First Secretary of the Moscow Committee of the Communist Party of the Soviet Union) from 1985–87, he was relieved from this post by Mikhail Gorbachev. After two years in the political wilderness, Mr Yeltsin was elected to the Supreme Soviet in March 1989, and in May 1990, he was elected

1.1.2   The Yeltsin economic reform programme

In October 1991, two months before the official end of the Soviet Union and two months after a failed conservative coup against the Gorbachev regime, Boris Yeltsin and his team of economic advisers, led by the liberal Yegor Gaidar (who was appointed Deputy Prime Minister and Minister of Economy and Finance) designed a programme of comprehensive economic reforms. The presidential team was granted special powers by the Supreme Soviet (still the upper legislative chamber) to implement these reforms.[10]

This (first) Yeltsin reform programme laid out a number of policy measures to achieve macroeconomic stabilisation (Mau & Starodubrovskaya, 2001; Neville, 2003). These included a planned sharp reduction in government spending (targeting mainly investment, defence and subsidies) to progressively reduce the government budget deficit from its very high 1991 level. The government launched new taxes and the tax collection system was to be overhauled to increase fiscal revenues. The programme also required the Central Bank of Russia (CBR) to cut subsidised credits to enterprises and to restrict money supply growth. A progressive reduction of inflation was projected, from the double-digit *monthly* levels observed in 1991. Additionally, the programme proposed the rapid creation of a *de novo* private sector, through a privatisation initiative[11] whose ultimate goal was to develop a new entrepreneurial, property-owning social class that would support the reform process (for a description of the Russian privatisation programme, see Box 1.1). In early 1992, the government lifted price controls on most consumer and intermediate goods.[12] It increased – but still controlled – prices on energy and food staples, e.g. bread, sugar and dairy products.

Chairman of the Presidium of the Supreme Soviet of the Russian Soviet Federative Socialist Republic (RSFSR). On 12 June 1991, he won the first direct presidential elections for the Russian Federation, taking office on 10 July 1991. He died on 23 April 2007, while this book was being written.

[10] The Yeltsin reform programme was complicated by the significant devolution of political and economic authority from the federal to the regional level, in a series of ad hoc agreements with Russia's many republics and other subnational authorities.

[11] Privatisation was allowed by the December 1991 Presidential Decree on Accelerating the Privatisation of State-Owned and Municipal Enterprises. The Supreme Soviet of Russia endorsed the Law of Privatisation in June 1992, which covered both medium-sized and large state-owned enterprises.

[12] Via the Presidential Decree on Lifting Price Controls of 12 January 1992.

Box 1.1 The Russian privatisation programme

The Russian privatisation programme was planned by Anatoly Borisovich Chubays, first Chairman of the State Committee for the Management of State Property during the first Yeltsin presidency (and current Chairman of the former electricity monopoly, RAO-UES). Its initial step was a voucher privatisation scheme, pushed by the Supreme Soviet against the wishes of Mr Chubays and Yegor Gaidar, who had wanted a direct sales privatisation from early on (Mau & Starodubrovskaya, 2001).

On 1 October 1992, vouchers, each with a nominal value of RUB 10,000 (or about $63), were distributed to the (then) 148 million citizens of the Russian Federation for the purchase of shares in medium-sized and large enterprises slated for privatisation. (Small enterprises were sold directly to interested investors; among other companies, banks were excluded from this privatisation process.) Voucher-holders could also sell the vouchers or invest in 'voucher funds'. Overnight this increased the private sector share in GDP by a factor of 5 (see Table B1.1).

At the end of June 1994, the voucher privatisation programme was completed. It succeeded in transferring ownership of 70% of Russia's large and medium-sized enterprises and in privatising about 90% of small enterprises, mostly to managers (and former workers) of those companies (which is usually referred to as an 'insiders' privatisation). By that time, 96% of the vouchers issued in 1992 had been used by their owners to buy shares in firms directly, invest in voucher funds or sell them on the secondary stock markets.

The next phase of the privatisation programme called for *direct* sales of the remaining state-owned enterprises, bringing in a much larger component of external control to the privatisation process, as 'red directors' were replaced by oligarchs. Since this met considerable opposition in the State Duma, President Yeltsin implemented it by a government decree on 1 July 1994. This second phase of the privatisation programme was completed by the first quarter of 1996. It significantly increased privatisation revenues (Table B1.1), but it has since been dogged by legal challenges. By February 1996, an investigation had already been launched into a 1995 transaction in which banks had awarded loans to the government in return for 'privatisep' shares in those enterprises (among the main beneficiaries were Menatep Bank, the financial arm of the group that will later become Yukos, and Oneximbank – see Appel, 1997). These loans-for-shares transactions were undertaken against the backdrop of an urgent need for budgetary revenue by the Russian government, but they also enabled truly phenomenal profits for a very limited number of individuals.

Box 1.1, cont.

The privatisation programme was halted from late 1995 to July 1996 during President Yeltsin's successful re-election campaign (assisted by the financial support of the oligarch class he had helped to create). From June 1996 onwards, the privatisation programme resumed, this time based on lists of specific, large state-owned enterprises to be sold through initial public offerings (IPOs). This action was enshrined in the July 1997 Law on the Privatisation of State-Owned Property and the Guidelines for Privatising Municipal Property in the Russian Federation. The heroic phase of the Russian (re)privatisation programme had already ended: in the space of only five years, the share of Russian GDP produced by the private sector had risen from close to 0 to around 70% (Table B1.1).

Table B1.1 **Privatisation revenues in Russia and the share of the private sector in GDP ($ billion)**

	1991	1992	1993	1994	1995	1996	1997	1998
Privatisation revenues	35	88	110	–	1,002	1,192	4,177	909
% of Russia in total privatisation revenues in Central and Eastern Europe and the CIS	1.37	2.43	2.76	0	10.3	21.8	25.3	11.4
Share of private sector in GDP (%)	5	25	40	50	55	60	70	70

Sources: European Bank for Reconstruction and Development (EBRD) and World Bank (2000).

Fundamental changes were made in the tax system. A value added tax was introduced on most transactions, and both a progressive income tax and a tax on enterprise revenues were established. The whole system of import and export tariffs was revised. New (higher) domestic energy prices were charged and new taxes on oil and natural gas exports were levied, seeking to narrow the gap between the (still subsidised to this day) domestic prices and world prices and to prevent domestic energy shortages. Most restrictions on foreign trade and investment were lifted (Kotz & Weir, 2007).[13]

---

[13] The elimination of the state monopoly over foreign trade was proclaimed by the Presidential Decree on Liberalisation of Foreign Economic Activity on the Territory of the Russian Soviet Federal Socialist Republic on 15 November 1991. Quotas on energy and raw material exports were kept. Although imports were liberalised, import duties were not initially established, as no such duties existed in the USSR.

1.1.3   A timeline of reform policies

Monetary policy in this newly created Russia was initially very accommodative. In January 1992, the government limited the growth of money supply[14] at the same time that most price controls were lifted.

Already by February 1992,[15] however, the CBR had resumed monetary expansion; by the end of 1992, the total Russian money supply had grown by around 18 times in nominal terms.

This very sharp increase in money supply was a reaction to the (necessary) post-liberalisation price adjustment, but it was also because of the absence of hard budget constraints in the still large state-owned sector. Banks (mostly state-owned) monetised interenterprise debts through their accounts and through their privileged access to the CBR (Owen & Robinson, 2003). Domestic credit aggregates reportedly grew by a factor of 9 between 1991 and 1992. This credit expansion was partially related to the CBR monetisation of interenterprise arrears: the government had limited the direct fiscal financing of state enterprises after January 1992, but they had reacted by building up arrears and interenterprise loans. By mid-1992, unpaid interenterprise loans had reached RUB 3.2 trillion (about $20 billion); the government later provided credit relief to those enterprises.

The government itself also failed to constrain its own expenditures, partially owing to the remaining influence of the Russian Supreme Soviet (which was violently dissolved in September 1993 and replaced by the new State Duma[16] in December of that year). At the end of 1992, the Russian budget deficit was close to 20% of GDP, or four times the projected share under the economic programme. This budget deficit was largely financed by monetary expansion, resulting in an inflation rate of over 2,500% in

---

[14] The CBR was then under the direct political control of the conservative Supreme Council of the Russian Federation (the parliament) and its Chairman, Ruslan Khasbulatov. Mr Khasbulatov was engaged in a political conflict with the reformist administration of President Yeltsin and he used the CBR as an instrument against the government's reforms and stabilisation policies.

[15] By that time, the IMF was advising the government and the CBR on preparing a joint policy programme (even before Russia's formal IMF membership, which occurred on 1 June 1992). This programme, however, did not include money growth targets, owing to the CBR's resistance.

[16] The Duma is the directly elected lower house of the Russian Federal Assembly, with the upper house being the Federation Council (which is made up of two members appointed by each region).

1992. These failures and the continuing conflict with the parliament led to the dismissal of the Gaidar cabinet and his replacement by the less reformist Viktor Stepanovich Chernomyrdin, an avuncular former head of the Ministry of the Gas Industry (MinGazProm, which would later become the notorious Gazprom company) and currently the Russian Ambassador in Ukraine.[17]

Nevertheless, Chernomyrdin appointed Boris Fedorov, perceived as a reformer, as Deputy Prime Minister and Finance Minister. In January 1993, Mr Fedorov announced plans for an 'anti-crisis programme' seeking to control inflation through tighter and consistent monetary and fiscal policies. Under the programme, the government would limit the budgetary financing of the deficit and close or privatise inefficient state-owned enterprises. Furthermore, the programme required the CBR to increase interest rates and reduce monetary financing. In May 1993, the Ministry of Finance and the CBR formally agreed to this stabilisation package. A new federal Constitution was approved by a referendum in December 1993, which strengthened the position of the presidency in its dealings with the State Duma (Kotz & Weir, 2007).

The 1993 stabilisation package had some early successes. In the first three quarters of 1993, the CBR reduced both money and credit creation.[18] As a result, the 1993 annual inflation rate fell to around 900% – still very high but a considerable improvement over 1992. Based on these early positive results, the International Monetary Fund (IMF) paid a first tranche of $1.5 billion to Russia from an agreed Systemic Transformation Facility in July 1993 (see Table 1.1), easing Russia's external position.[19]

---

[17] Yegor Timurovich Gaidar remained in the government until December 1992, and then returned from September 1993 until January 1994 as First Deputy Prime Minister. The son and grandson of high Soviet *nomenklatura* (his father was a rear admiral, his grandfather a famous Bolshevik writer), after leaving government Yegor Gaidar founded a reformist political party (the Union of Right Forces) and was elected as a deputy in the State Duma between 1999 and 2003. After leaving the Duma, he concentrated on his academic activities (he is currently President of an economic think tank, the Institute for the Economy in Transition).

[18] Some of this improvement was brought about by a further build-up of interenterprise arrears in 1993.

[19] The Systemic Transformation Facility was created in April 1993, to enable the IMF to lend to countries in transition from centrally planned to market economies *before* they started implementing macro stabilisation and structural reforms.

Table 1.1 IMF lending to Russia, by type of arrangement and value (in $ million)

Type of arrangement	IMF Board approval date	Amount approved	Amount disbursed
Stand-by Arrangement (1st tranche)	05/08/1992	1,047.2	1,047.2
Systemic Transformation Facility (1st tranche)	30/06/1993	1,513.1	1,513.1
Systemic Transformation Facility (2nd tranche)	22/03/1994	1,522.8	1,522.8
Stand-by Arrangement (1st tranche)	11/04/1995	6,798.2	6,798.2
Extended Fund Facility	26/03/1996	10,083.8	7,459.5
Extended Fund Facility Augmentation	20/07/1998	1,659.2	–
Supplemental Reserve Facility	20/07/1998	5,307.3	897.4
Compensation and Contingent Financing Facility	20/07/1998	2,867.7	2,867.7
Stand-by Arrangement	28/07/1999	4,501.9	642.5
Total	–	35,301.1	22,748.3

Source: IMF.

In mid-1994, the Chernomyrdin government presented an additional reform package to parliament, which was again undermined by the CBR and by pressure groups lobbying the State Duma for subsides. This outcome led to further inflationary pressures and a run on the ruble during October 1994 – on a single day, 11 October 1994 (dubbed 'Black Tuesday'), the ruble dropped by 27%.

President Yeltsin reacted to this by firing Viktor Vladimirovich Gerashchenko,[20] who had been head of the CBR since the late 1980s (when the CBR had still been the state bank of the Soviet Union, Gosbank) and nominating Tatiana Paramonova as his replacement. She implemented tighter monetary and credit policies, and introduced a harder exchange rate regime (see section 1.4.3). This was supported by a 1995 parliamentary act that restricted the monetary financing of the budget, while the Ministry of Finance began to issue government bonds to finance the deficit. The 1995 budget draft – presented to the Duma in September 1994 – included a further commitment to curtail 'soft budget constraints' in state-owned

---

[20] At that time, infamously described as the "worst Central Banker in history" by Harvard's Jeffrey Sachs, who was an adviser to the Russian government between November 1991 and January 1994.

enterprises. Another IMF programme supporting the new reform package was negotiated in April 1995, to shore up the external position of Russia (Table 1.1).

Nevertheless, the electoral cycle (parliamentary elections were scheduled for December 1995, and presidential elections for mid-1996) caused fiscal easing pressures to reappear in late 1995. This situation led to the replacement of some of the remaining key reformists in the Yeltsin economic team (Tatiana Paramonova,[21] who was replaced in November 1995 by Sergey Dubinin, while Anatoly Chubays left his position as First Deputy Prime Minister in January 1996). President Yeltsin was re-elected in the second round of voting on 3 June 1996. Yet the combination of his weakening health (he had had a heart attack during the campaign), the political (and financial) compromises that he had made during the electoral campaign towards the oligarchs (who had supported him against a candidate fielded by the Communist Party) and the upcoming crisis would limit his drive for further reforms.

1.2   The period 1997–98, or a crisis forewarned

The year 1997 started well for Russia: for the first time since the late 1980s, positive growth was observed (1.4%), inflation was falling from the dizzying 1992 heights to below 15% a year and a new (harder) exchange rate regime was providing a nominal anchor for expectations (Owen & Robinson, 2003). In September 1997, Russia was allowed to join the Paris Club after rescheduling the payment of over $60 billion in Soviet debt to other governments. Another agreement for a 23-year debt repayment of $33 billion was signed a month later with the London Club, this one concerning debts to private banks (Chiodo & Owyang, 2002). Additionally, limitations on the purchase of government securities by non-resident investors were removed, facilitating foreign investment in Russia: by late 1997, non-residents were responsible for around 30% of the GKO[22] market.[23] But this

---

[21] Ms Paramonova returned to the CBR in 1998, with the post-crisis team led by Mr Gerashchenko, and was among its Deputy Chairpersons until September 2007, when she became the Presidential Representative at the Russian National Banking Council.

[22] GKO refers to the most common short-term Russian government Treasury bill (*Gosudarstvennoe Kratkosrochnoe Obyazatelstvo*).

apparent *relative* stabilisation was misleading, as several weaknesses lurked under a seemingly benign environment (Owen & Robinson, 2003).

One was Russia's *low rate of tax collection*,[24] which caused the public sector deficit to remain very high (see section 1.4.5). The majority of tax revenues came from taxes that were linked to a limited number of products, therefore exposing the Russian fiscal position to notoriously unstable commodity prices. Furthermore, given the new constitutional federal settlement under President Yeltsin, the revenue from most taxes was now shared between the federal and regional governments. This fiscal fragility was clearly reflected in the continually very high budget deficits, which almost hit 10% of GDP in 1996 and were above 8% in 1997 (see Figure 1.8 in section 1.4.5).

Another weakness was *contagion*. In the summer of 1997, the Asian crisis caused an across-the-board reduced appetite for emerging-market assets among investors. In November 1997, after its onset, the ruble came under pressure (see section 1.4.3). The CBR was initially successful in defending the currency, albeit by losing nearly $6 billion (or around a third) from its foreign reserves. At the same time, non-resident holders of GKOs started signing forward contracts with Russian banks to exchange rubles for US dollars, which enabled them to hedge their exchange rate risks (forward-looking markets were already pricing in ruble devaluation).

Another weakness – related to contagion, as similarly harder regimes faced comparable pressures – was also one of the apparent strengths of the Russian position: *the exchange rate regime*. The sliding peg prevented a nominal depreciation to correct fully for the still substantial inflation differential, resulting in persistent real appreciation (see Figure 1.6 in section 1.4.3). This situation fostered the *expectation* of devaluation, while the exchange rate framework itself provided speculators with the potential for profits through 'one-sided' positions against the currency.

---

[23] John Odling-Smee, former Director of the IMF European II Department, which had covered the Soviet Union (in the 2000s, the European II Department disappeared: its portfolio of countries was divided and merged into other IMF geographical divisions), indicates that this liberalisation of the Russian capital market *may have been premature* and *may* have contributed to the 1998 crisis. He also maintains that the IMF *should* have warned Russia about this (see Odling-Smee, 2004).

[24] In 1995, fiscal revenue plus grants was a mere 16% of GDP. By 1998, it had fallen below 12%.

Finally, the low point of the previous *energy price cycle* was about to be reached: in December 1997, the price of crude oil began to drop, putting additional pressure on Russia's external position (see section 1.5.2).

Matters came to a head during 1998, as new signs of inconsistent economic policies appeared. In February 1998, the Russian government submitted a proposal for a new tax code to the State Duma that was only approved later in the year, and in a much weaker version. Political risk also increased during 1998: unexpectedly, on 23 March 1998, Boris Yeltsin fired his entire government and appointed Sergei Vladilenovich Kiriyenko, a relatively unknown figure, as the new Prime Minister. He was not confirmed in the post by the Duma until after an entire month, during which there was a policy vacuum. In early April, the CBR head, Sergei Dubinin, made public statements concerning an *upcoming* debt crisis, which were – almost on cue – followed by statements by Mr Kiriyenko about fiscal revenue shortfalls expected for 1998.

Not surprisingly, the markets started pricing in a 'default risk' in Russian assets. By 18 May 1998, government bond yields had reached almost 50%; they would rise even further later in the month. The CBR had to increase its lending rate to a matching level, and in two days lost a further $1 billion of reserves defending the ruble from another attack. In June, the CBR was forced to raise its rate to 150%, and lost another $5 billion in reserves. Meanwhile, oil prices had dropped to a historical low of $11 per barrel (see Figure 1.10 and section 1.5.2).

Still in June, the government proposed a new 'anticrisis plan' to the State Duma, with added revenue-raising measures. The Duma weakened these provisions, limiting the additional expected RUB 71 billion in revenue to a trifling RUB 3 billion (Chiodo & Owyang, 2002).

By that time, the external position of Russia had become very difficult: $3 billion in loans were due by late September 1998, in addition to the estimated several billions of US dollar/ruble futures swaps that were due later in the year. In July, the IMF approved a further assistance package worth around $10 billion, of which $4.8 billion was to be disbursed immediately. But this was just not enough to cover the entire expected external shortfall. (See Table 1.1 above for a timetable of all IMF programmes in Russia. It should be noted that these figures in no way represent the whole 'envelope' of external finance made available by the international community to Russia, which also included bilateral credits and grants, along with loans and grants from other international financial institutions such as the World Bank and the European Commission, including ECFIN.)[25]

On 13 August 1998, the Russian stock, bond and currency markets collapsed as a result of investor fears. Annual yields on ruble-denominated bonds skyrocketed, and the stock market had to be closed for trading after precipitous falls in the indexes.[26]

Finally, on 17 August 1998 the Russian government formally let go of the hard exchange-rate framework, removing the exchange rate band and ultimately devaluing the ruble by over 70%. It defaulted on its domestic debt and declared a three-month moratorium on payments by commercial banks to foreign creditors. The whole government was sacked on 23 August,[27] including the head of the CBR.[28] A comprehensive policy response to the crisis was not forthcoming, however; a fiscal package did

---

[25] Some commentators (see Bluestein, 2001) question the usefulness of this last IMF programme. The IMF (see Odling-Smee, 2004) defends the package on the grounds that there was nothing essentially unsustainable about the Russian situation in the run-up to the 1998 crisis. Nevertheless, Odling-Smee (2004) refers to pressure from the G7 towards a more 'lenient' treatment of Russia. In any case, that was one of the last occasions on which the IMF had a meaningful influence on the economic policy debate in Russia. With the resumption of growth in the late 1990s/early 2000s, the importance for Russia (and for other emerging markets) of the IMF and of its sister institution, the World Bank, would be significantly reduced (which was demonstrated by the IMF's planned personnel reduction announced in late 2007). Arguably, the international body with the highest level of influence and leverage in the policy debate in Russia today is that often-underestimated organisation, the European Commission.

[26] From January to August 1998, the stock market lost more than 75% of its value – 39% in May alone.

[27] Sergei Kiriyenko was replaced by Viktor Chernomyrdin (whose appointment was twice rejected by the State Duma, leading to a government headed by Yevgeny Primakov). Mr Kiriyenko later became the head of the Union of Right Forces Party, and afterwards President Vladimir Putin's envoy to the Volga Federal District. In 2005, he was appointed head of Rosatom, the Russian Federal Atomic Energy Agency.

[28] Peculiarly, Sergei Dubinin (who left government for the first time in 1994, because of his involvement in the Black Tuesday debacle, and who is now Deputy Chairman of RAO-UES) was replaced in 1998 by Viktor Gerashchenko, who would remain Chairman of the CBR until his retirement in 2002 (for age reasons, having turned 65 that year).

not appear until 1999, while the CBR acted to assure liquidity and the integrity of the payments and banking systems, also using the state-owned banks as tools for that purpose. Russia's first transition had ended in tears.

1.3 Lessons from Russia's first transition

The initial stabilisation and economic reform processes in Russia during the 1990s cannot be considered a failure, as they more or less comprehensively implemented the fundamental institutions necessary for a market economy and largely opened up and integrated the Russian economy into the wider global economy. The Russian policy-makers who came later on would essentially 'only' have to finish this work.

Nevertheless, these reforms were clearly incomplete and their weaknesses were graphically revealed by the 1998 collapse. There were many microeconomic deficiencies in the Russian reforms (such as an imperfect privatisation and incomplete price liberalisation, notably in the domestic energy sector), but the underlying causes of the 1998 crisis were mostly macroeconomic (again, admittedly with microeconomic underpinnings): an inconsistent policy mix, an unsustainable exchange rate regime and a lax fiscal stance.

Together, these elements made the Russian economy very vulnerable to external shocks, and when the combined shocks of the Asian crisis (which reduced the risk appetite of foreign investors towards emerging markets across the board) and the historically very low oil prices hit during 1997–98, the result was a full-blown, almost textbook-perfect external sustainability crisis. The Russian crisis itself was part of a long series of similar crises throughout the 1990s, linked to the fundamentally unsustainable nature of a hard(er) exchange rate regime without a consistent policy mix in an environment of liberalised capital flows. These crises included the 1992–93 travails of the Exchange Rate Mechanism I (ERM-I) in the EU, the 1994 Mexican collapse, the 1997 Asian crisis, the 1999 Brazilian turmoil and 2001 Argentinian experience.

A subsequent section deals with the current Russian growth model and discusses how well lessons from the first transition have been learned. Yet before that, the next section presents in more detail the developments in the main macroeconomic aggregates during the 1990s and beyond.

1.4 Macro performance during Russia's transitions

This section presents a description of the main macro variables since the beginning of transition in Russia. The next section (1.5) will analyse those developments in more detail, concentrating on the more recent trends.

1.4.1 GDP performance

Economic data around the immediate USSR dissolution period[29] is often very unreliable. The difficulty lies in the sometimes very severe information deficiencies and the lack of reliable market exchange rates, which limits the validity of international comparisons. In any case, a very significant fall in Russian GDP during the years immediately before *and* after the end of the Soviet Union can be observed (see Figure 1.1).

Figure 1.1 GDP growth rates in Russia (%)

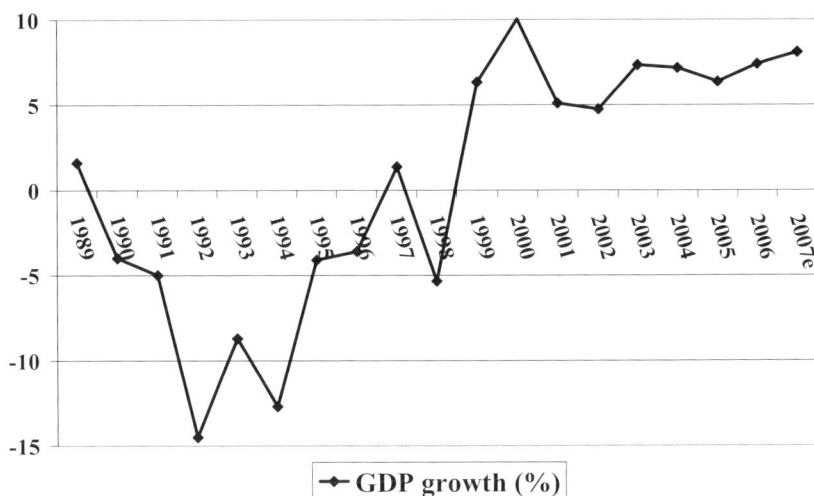

Sources: World Bank's World Development Indicators (WDI) and Russian Federal State Statistics Service (Rosstat).

Successive years of negative growth continued until 1996, with a brief period of positive growth in 1997, followed by the sharp post-crisis downturn of 1998. Still, it should be noted that even those several years of

---

[29] This period covers 1990–92, as some of the USSR republics had effectively declared themselves sovereign in 1990, while others had initially been reluctant to declare independence even after the formal dissolution of the Union.

negative growth were a *necessary* step for the return to positive growth rates. This is to be expected, as necessarily the introduction of market-based institutions and the consequent reorganisation of the economy is not an instantaneous process. Using nominal exchange rates also paints a very stark picture of the development of the Russian economy: in 1989, Russian nominal GDP was around $500 billion, but fell *below* $200 billion in 1999 and then jumped almost sevenfold to nearly $1.4 trillion by 2007. On the other hand, using the more adequate benchmark of GDP in purchasing power parity (PPP) terms, which takes into account the different costs of a standardised consumption basket among countries, Russia's economic performance is much less dramatic and follows a somewhat different path. A mild U-shape can be observed, in which the nadir occurred in 1998, but GDP *never* fell below 58% of the 1989 height. Furthermore, by 2006 it had roughly returned to its 1989 level (see Figures 1.2 and 1.3). [30]

Figure 1.2 Russian GDP and GDP in PPP ($ billion)

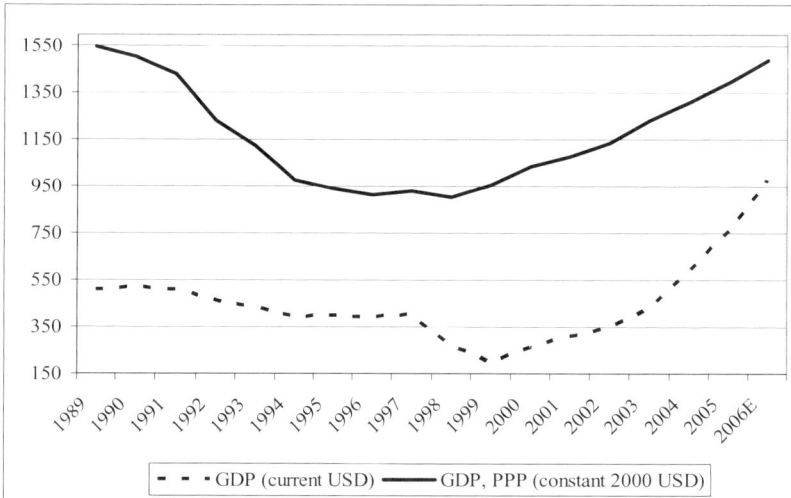

Sources: WDI and Rosstat.

The same picture holds true for GDP *per capita*: using an index based on 1989, in 2006, Russian GDP in PPP per capita had approximately

---

[30] Åslund (2001) estimates that when one takes into consideration other factors (such as unreported or undercounted economic activities), Russian GDP had reached 94% of its 1989 value by 1995, implying a comparatively marginal fall of 6%.

reached its 1989 level (albeit when one uses GDP in PPP per capita calculated using *current* instead of *constant* international US dollars, the 1989 level had been reached by 2002, and now stands at around 150% of it). On the other hand, the GDP recovery of Russia relative to its 1989 level still lags behind that experienced by the new EU member states – although it is roughly comparable to that observed in the south-eastern European transition countries and is also at the level of the aggregate performance of the Commonwealth of Independent States (CIS) (see Figure 1.3).

Figure 1.3 GDP index measures (base year 1989)

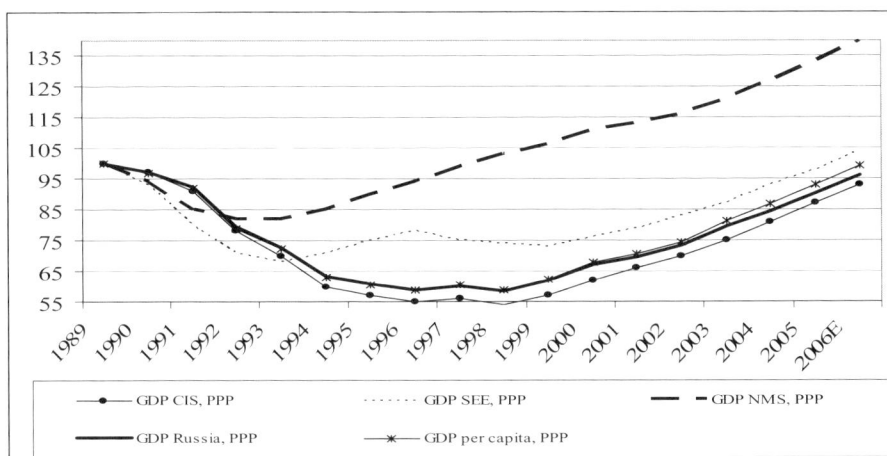

Notes: NMS = new member states; SEE = south-eastern European transition countries.
Sources: WDI and EBRD.

This outcome stems from the fact that while Russia's initial growth performance was clearly below the aggregate of all transition countries[31] (i.e. all the previously centrally planned economies of Central and Eastern Europe and the Balkans), from 1999 onwards, that has no longer been the

---

[31] As a rule, *all* transition countries experienced several years of negative growth, referred to in the literature as the 'transition recession'. This period of negative GDP growth is linked to the necessary time to reorganise the existing factors of production according to their marginal productivities and the international comparative advantage of the individual countries (see Vinhas de Souza & Havrylyshyn, 2006). It is also related to the *depth* of accumulated distortions: as the Soviet Union had been under a planned economic system for a generation longer than Eastern Europe, the distortions there (for instance, the degree of over-industrialisation) were more serious. See Åslund (2001) and Kornai (1994).

case (see Figure 1.4). Since 1999, Russia's performance has been quite close to the CIS[32] and all transition averages, and has actually surpassed the performance of the new member states.[33]

Figure 1.4 Comparative GDP growth rates (%)

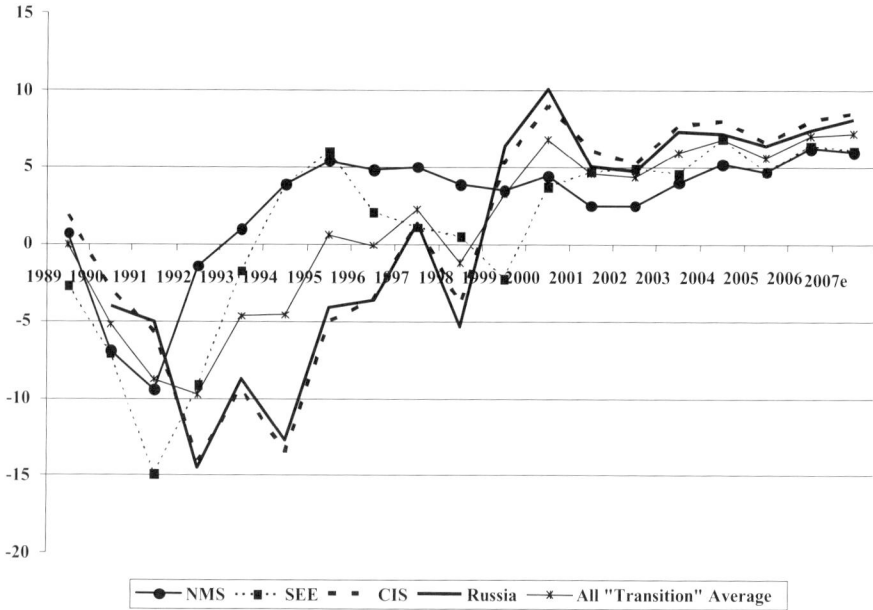

Source: EBRD.

1.4.2 Inflation

In 1992, the first year of major economic reform, the consumer price index (CPI) in Russia increased by a whopping 2,520%. A major cause of the

---

[32] The CIS average in Figure 1.4 is GDP-weighted. As Russian GDP represents between 75% and 80% of the total GDP of the CIS, Russia's growth performance strongly determines the CIS performance. Using a reference of the CIS minus Russia, Russia was below this benchmark between 1996 and 1998 and after 2001.

[33] As one can see in Figure 1.4, the transitional recession in the new member states occurred before that in the CIS countries, as they began the transition process earlier than the CIS did – some as early as in the 1980s. This reveals another problem when comparing growth performance (or indeed, progress in reforms) between the CIS and other regions. Some works adjust the comparison by basing series on the first year of transition (termed 'transition time').

increase was the deregulation of most of the prices in January 1992: the CPI index increased in that month *alone* by 245%. This price shock was a positive, one-off non-monetary move that reflected the *necessary and beneficial* adjustment to world price levels. In 1993, the annual inflation rate had declined to 875%, which was still a very high figure; by 1994, it had fallen to just over 300%. In 1996, it was already below 50% yearly, and it fell to around 15% in 1997 (see Figure 1.5). A brief inflationary, post-devaluation spike occurred in 1999, after which inflation decreased to single digits in 2006, then returned to low double digits in 2007. As one might see, this trajectory roughly mirrors the one observed in the CIS average, albeit the deflationary process was much faster in the CEE countries.

Figure 1.5 CPI, pre- and post-1998

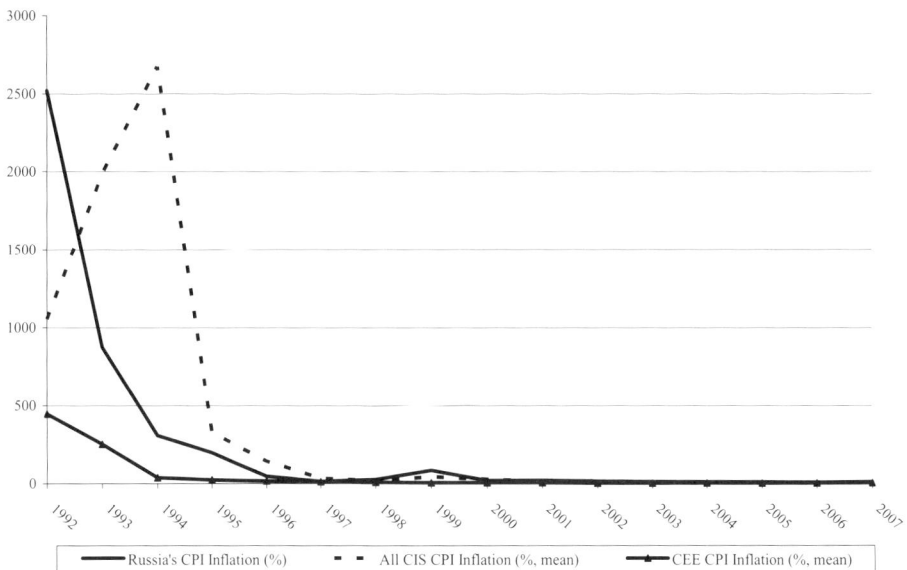

Source: IMF.

These yearly averages mask substantial variations of the monthly inflation rates, linked to normal seasonality (for instance, the infamous, bitterly cold Russian winters, which affect food prices) and punctual 'policy' shocks from the Russian monetary and fiscal authorities throughout the early to mid-1990s. In any case, the overall picture is clear: a rather steady but slow disinflation process.

1.4.3   Exchange rate dynamics

The dissolution of the Soviet Union did not immediately lead to the establishment of a truly *Russian* monetary authority capable of conducting an independent monetary policy,[34] as, until mid-1993, some of the former republics of the Soviet Union still used the ruble, and the central banks of those republics conducted their *own* policy simultaneously with the CBR. Only after 1993 did the CBR really start to conduct a *national* – and initially loose – monetary policy. During the period from July 1992, when the (now) Russian ruble could be legally exchanged for US dollars, to August 1998, the official exchange rate for the ruble/US dollar declined from RUB 1 per $1 to around RUB 7.9 (see Figure 1.6; prior to July 1992, the ruble rate had been set at a highly overvalued level).

Figure 1.6 Exchange rate developments

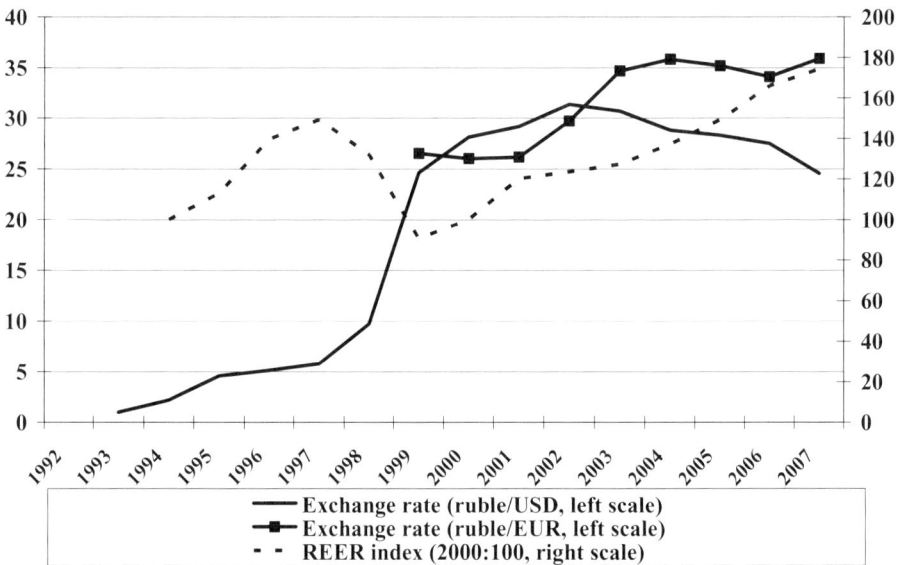

Legend:
— Exchange rate (ruble/USD, left scale)
—■— Exchange rate (ruble/EUR, left scale)
- - REER index (2000:100, right scale)

Source: IMF.

---

[34] The CBR was founded on 13 July 1990, based on the Russian Republic Bank of the State Bank of the Soviet Union (the former Gosbank). On 2 December 1990, the Supreme Soviet of the RSFSR passed the Law on the Central Bank of the RSFSR (Bank of Russia), which declared the CBR a legal entity and the main bank of the Russian Federation.

This loose monetary stance continued until the middle of 1995, when the Russian economy started showing signs of stabilisation and a new CBR law was passed, providing the CBR with a greater degree of legal independence in conducting monetary policy.

This change allowed the CBR to adopt a tighter monetary policy and to introduce a pegged exchange-rate regime with a crawling band against the US dollar, which replaced the previous 'dirty float' from July 1995 onwards: the CBR announced its intention to maintain the ruble within a band of 4.300 to 4.900 per $1 through mid-1996.[35] The announcement reflected strengthened fiscal and monetary policies and the build-up of reserves with which the CBR could defend the ruble. A direct consequence of this harder exchange-rate regime was an increase in the real effective exchange rate (REER), given the still substantial inflation differential between Russia and its main trading partners.

As a result of these measures, inflation slowed down further (see Figure 1.5 above). Furthermore, because of favourable developments in the local securities market, direct credit to the government significantly decreased and the CBR started to conduct monetary policy through indirect instruments, such as interest rates and reserve requirements. Yet the start of the Asian crisis of 1997 spread a negative shock throughout emerging markets. This external shock reduced investment confidence in Russia and caused capital outflows, forcing the CBR to defend the band of a rapidly appreciating currency: by late 1997, the ruble had experienced a real appreciation of almost 50% when compared with 1994 (see Figure 1.6, above). After two rounds of further attacks during 1998, the collapse of the framework was to follow. It was replaced by an informal US dollar (and later basket) targeting. With the boom in oil prices from 1999 onwards, REER appreciation pressures reappeared, bringing it back to its pre-crisis level by 2005.

1.4.4 External position

Remarkably, Russia's trade balance was *always* positive throughout the 1990s: even at the low point of the oil price cycle in 1997–98, Russia was registering trade surpluses of at least $15 billion yearly.

---

[35] The ruble would later undergo a redenomination in early 1998 that would cut three zeroes from its face value.

Also somewhat surprisingly, the current account was *never* in significant deficit – even during 1997–98, it was effectively in balance and it was strongly positive in most of the other years (see Figure 1.7).

Figure 1.7 External developments

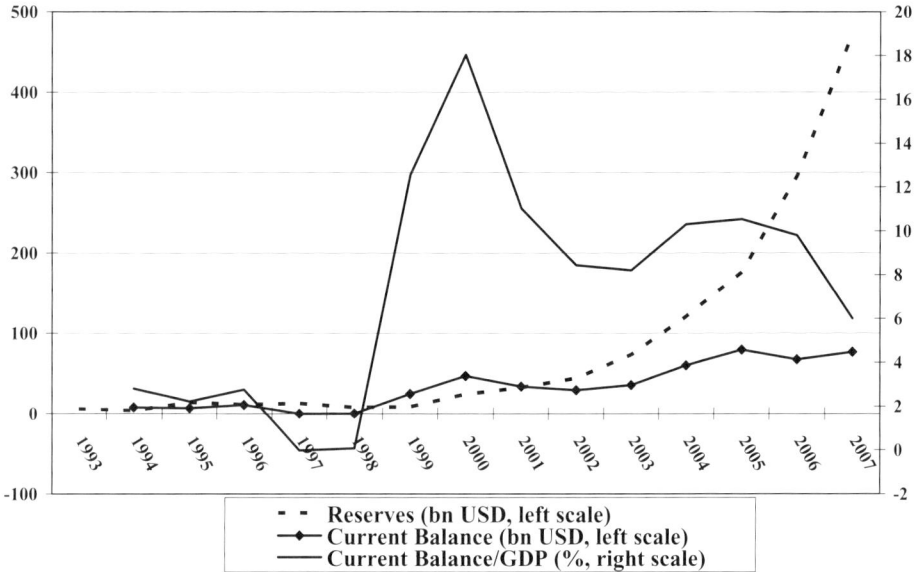

Source: IMF.

1.4.5 Fiscal position

Figure 1.8 reveals the true Achilles' heel of the Russian macroeconomic policy until 1998: *the fragility of its fiscal position*. For this entire period, fiscal deficits of up to 10% of GDP (or even more) were the rule (albeit the average CIS performance was even worse than that).

As indicated earlier, this state of affairs stemmed from the significant dependency of Russia on taxes linked to commodity prices, especially energy ones and the imperfect nature of the fiscal pact between the Federation and the regions enshrined by the 1993 Constitution. Other contributing factors were the unwillingness of the government to enforce hard budget constraints in the formerly state-owned enterprises and the relations between the Russian government and the new industrial groups, which frequently enabled oligarchs to negotiate ad hoc tax treatment.

Figure 1.8 Balance of the federal government budget

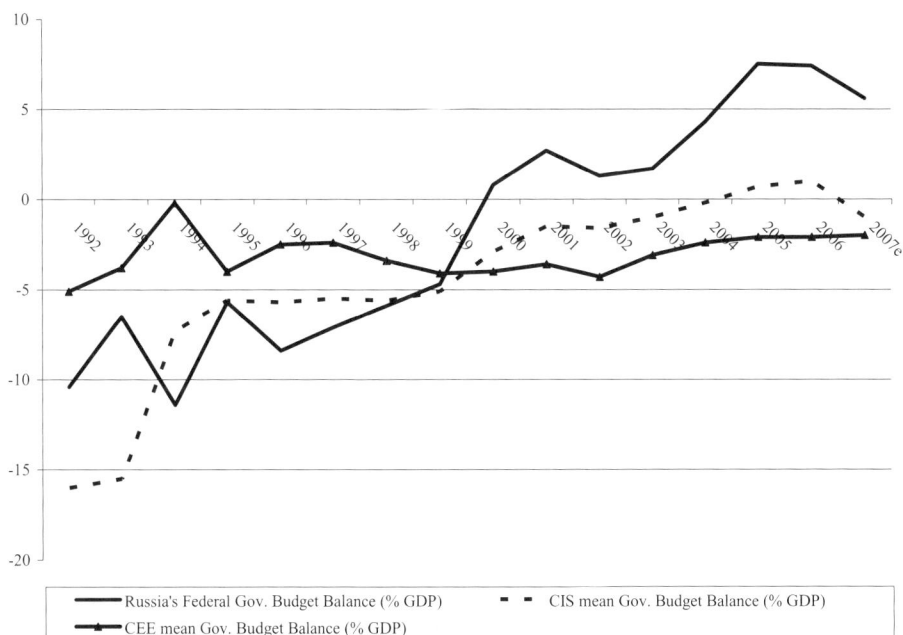

Source: IMF.

The post-2000 oil boom, plus significant reforms in the macro framework, would completely change the fiscal stance, to one of consistent and high headline fiscal surpluses.

1.5 Post-1998 macroeconomic performance

Confounding most international and domestic observers, Russia's macro performance after the 1998 debacle has been nothing short of impressive. While the average growth rate for the period 1990–98 was a dismal -6.3%,[36] the average growth rate for the period 1999-2007 was a robust +7% (Rosstat's 2007 growth estimate for Russia is 8.1%).[37]

---

[36] One must note that this performance is actually better than the CIS average (non-GDP weighted) for the same period, which was -6.8%. As a comparator, the average GDP growth for the new EU member states for the same period was a 'mere' -1.7%.

[37] As 7% yearly growth is what is necessary for the doubling of a GDP in 10 years, President Putin's promise to do so is now within sight.

The growth drivers for these two periods were fundamentally different. As indicated in the previous section, a period of negative growth is inevitably associated with the introduction of market economy institutions. The only question concerning this earlier transformation stage is what kinds of frameworks can mitigate and shorten it.[38]

Once market economy institutions are in place, a more proper discussion of growth drivers is possible. That is indeed the case for Russia post-1998. At the same time, clear differences can be distinguished among the growth drivers for the sub-periods *after* 1998. Here, *three phases of growth* between 1999 and 2006 are broadly differentiated (following Owen & Robinson, 2003 and Ahrend, 2006), including indications that a new phase may have started in 2006:

1) In the immediate aftermath of the 1998 crisis (1999–2000), growth was mainly driven by the *competitiveness gains from the ruble devaluation.*

2) *Energy price increases* during 2001–06 along with a significant rise in *oil production* (at least until 2004) drove growth in the second period. In conjunction with these trends, from 2004 onwards a *consumption boom* can be observed (supported by terms-of-trade gains arising from energy exports and later from an increase in fiscal expenditures).

3) In 2006, with the pick-up of investment, an *investment-led growth phase* may have begun in Russia.

Beyond the underlying factors listed above, the cumulative importance of – even if limited and incomplete – *structural reform* and a more robust *macro policy mix* have also been crucial for growth resumption.

1.5.1   1999–2000

The Russian economy recovered surprisingly quickly from the 1998 crisis. Between 1998 and 1999, Russia experienced a truly significant fiscal adjustment, as the federal fiscal deficit fell from 8.1% to 3.1% of GDP (and turned into a surplus by 2000). These changes were partly automatic, as the newly increased inflation reduced real (non-indexed) expenditures, while (indexed) real revenues rose (Owen & Robinson, 2003). Meanwhile, imports fell sharply, as their prices more than tripled in ruble terms.

---

[38] A usual conclusion of the transition literature is that more robust macro and institutional frameworks (such as those provided by the EU accession processes) are quite effective in reducing these adjustment costs (see Vinhas de Souza, 2004a).

Correspondingly, the current account surplus grew very rapidly (from 0.1% of GDP in 1998 to a massive 12.6% of GDP in 1999).

This quick recovery was made possible by the existence of unused installed capacity and by the limited domestic significance of the banking system (one of the sectors most affected by the 1998 crisis) in terms of domestic financing, which limited the negative spin-offs from the banking collapse. Industrial production increased again in October 1998 and by March 1999, it had surpassed its December 1997 level (see Figure 1.9, in which the substantial post-1998 jump is clearly visible).

Figure 1.9 Monthly industrial production index (1993=100)

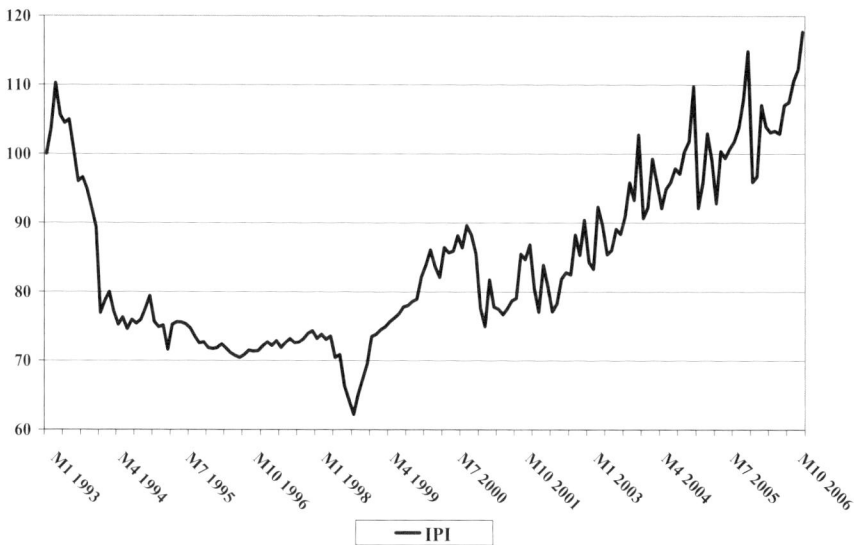

Source: Rosstat.

Growth was very broadly spread across industrial sectors, including non-resource ones, both domestically and internationally oriented (see Table 1.2). After the textbook-perfect crisis, this was an equally textbook-perfect example of a considerable 'expenditure switching' from imports to domestic goods caused by a (real) devaluation. The large initial decline in input costs (real wages and energy prices, the latter a *deliberate* policy decision by the Russian government) enabled Russian industry to become competitive again both at home and abroad, while the depreciation priced some imports out of the market.

Table 1.2 Contribution of sectors to industrial production growth (%)

	1996	1997	1998	1999	2000	2001	2002	2003	2004
Electrical power	-4.6	-16.7	-4.0	-1.2	1.4	2.2	-0.8	0.7	0.2
Fuel industry (oil, gas, coal)	-17.3	19.3	-47.3	18.1	28.1	53.7	65.4	61.7	57.6
Ferrous metallurgy	-3.4	6.3	-12.5	14.4	9.7	-0.2	3.1	6.4	4.4
Nonferrous metallurgy	-11.0	59.5	-10.3	14.6	14.7	8.5	10.6	7.7	5.3
Chemical and petro-chemical industry	-8.8	7.6	-5.7	12.7	5.2	4.8	1.2	2.1	4.2
Machine-building industry	-13.4	38.1	-21.8	22.2	18.6	11.8	3.6	11.3	17.3
Wood and paper industry	-21.6	3.6	0.4	10.4	5.4	2.1	1.7	0.7	1.7
Building materials industry	-13.2	-9.7	-3.4	3.1	2.7	2.2	1.1	1.7	1.6
Light industry	7.0	1.9	2.2	-1.4	-1.7	-0.7	0.5	0.2	0.8
Food industry	-13.7	-9.9	2.4	7.1	15.8	15.6	13.5	7.5	6.9

Source: Rosstat.

1.5.2   2001–05

From 2001 onwards, a fundamental difference began to appear in the Russian growth drivers, with the increased prominence of the energy sector (i.e. including oil, gas and coal). Its contribution to overall industrial growth almost doubled from 2000 to 2001, from 28% to 54% (Table 1.2). This change occurred on the back of significant increases in oil and gas prices (see Figure 1.10).

In 1998, oil prices[39] (crude oil was one of the most important Russian export products, even during Soviet times)[40] had fallen to the historically

---

[39] Gas prices also tend to move in tandem with oil prices, with a lag of a few months.

very low average price of $12.7 per barrel of UK Brent crude. As a comparison, this price was not only nearly *half* the crude price in 1990, but was also significantly below the post-war nominal average price of $15.1. In contrast, by late 2000, oil prices had surpassed $28 per barrel, *more than 120% higher than their 1998 low.*

Figure 1.10 Oil and gas prices ($)

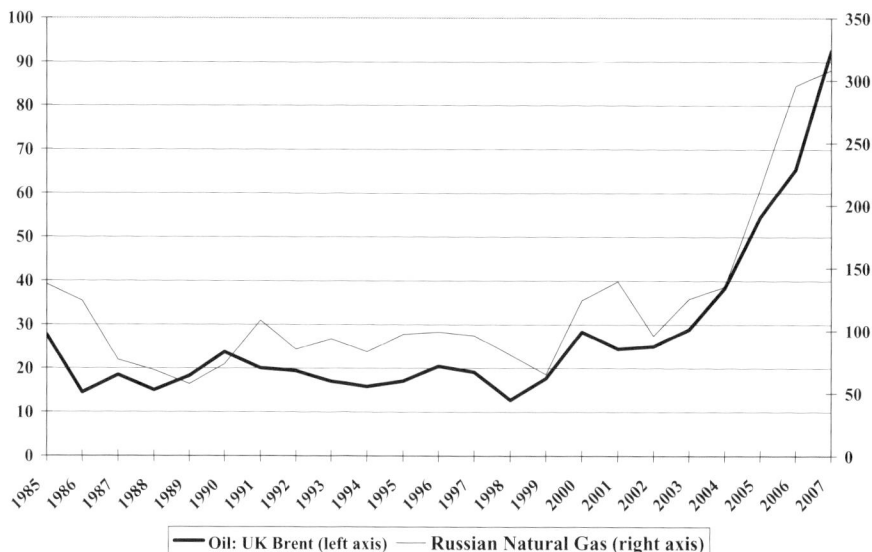

Source: IMF.

The effects of these changes were dramatic. The value of total Russian exports barely increased between 1998 and 1999, but the share of oil in total exports jumped from less than a quarter to around a third. In 2000, the value of total exports rose by almost 40%, climbing above $100 billion for

---

[40] The discovery and exploration of significant oil and gas fields in the early 1970s enabled a temporary increase of the USSR's growth rates. It also markedly extended the degree of openness of the Soviet economy, with energy products quickly reaching over 50% of the total exports by value by the late 1970s (Mau & Starodubrovskaya, 2001). Differentiated interests emerged within the Soviet *nomenklatura* concerning economic relations with the wider world. Some authors (ibid.) even partially blame the fall of the Soviet Union itself on the reduction in oil prices that occurred during the 1980s.

the first time, while the share of oil came close to 40%. The consequent current account surplus was a huge 18% of GDP in 2000 and was to average 11% of GDP for the whole period 2000–06 (see Table 1.3).[41] The EU is largely responsible for this surplus, being by far the largest trading and investment partner of Russia: in 2006, it was responsible for 63% of Russia's exports, but for just 51% of its imports (or around 60% of total trade).

Table 1.3 Imports, exports and the current account surplus

	1999	2000	2001	2002	2003	2004	2005	2006
Exports ($ billion)	75.6	105	101.9	107.3	135.9	183.5	243.6	302.3
Imports ($ billion)	39.5	44.9	53.8	61	76.1	96.3	125.3	162.7
Current account ($ billion)	24.6	46.8	33.9	29.1	35.4	60.1	83.3	95.6
Current account (% of GDP)	12.7	18	11	8.5	8.2	10.3	11.2	9.8
Trade balance (% of GDP)	18.4	23.2	15.8	11	11	12	14	12.6

Sources: Author's estimations, based on CBR, Rosstat and IMF.

This export performance was not just the result of energy price increases. The 1999–2004 *supply response* of the Russian energy industry (and especially the oil sector) was quite considerable. This response can be seen in Table 1.4, which plots the terms of trade against nominal exports.

Table 1.4 Terms of trade and nominal export indexes (2001=100)

	2001	2002	2003	2004	2005	2006
Terms of trade index (2001=100)	100	103	113	128	148	159
Export index (in nominal $, 2001=100)	100	105	133	180	239	298

Sources: Author's estimations, based on CBR and Rosstat.

---

[41] The sterilisation of these very substantial hard currency inflows was to create a situation of almost permanent excess liquidity in the Russian money market. Consequently, real short-term interest rates have usually been negative, thus limiting the usefulness of the usual central bank instruments of monetary policy.

Following the demise of the Soviet Union in 1991, oil production fell substantially, reaching a bottom of roughly 6 million barrels per day (mbd) or around half of the Soviet-era peak in 1986. A turnaround in Russian oil output began in 1999, *caused by the earlier privatisation of the industry*, beyond the rising world oil prices (the structure of the Russian energy industry is described in Box 1.2). This rebound has continued since 1999, resulting in a total production in 2007 of 9.87 mbd – over 62% more than the 1998 level, albeit at diminishing rates in 2005–07.[42]

A somewhat similar process has also been observed in the gas industry, but with much smaller growth rates in production. The 2007 production reached 653 billion cubic metres (bcm) or only 14% above the low point observed in 1997 (see Table 1.5). These different performances stem from variations in the *industrial structures* under which the industries operate (with that for oil being a relatively competitive and for the most part privately owned oligopoly versus the state-owned monopoly for gas) as well as in the related *regulatory frameworks* (with world level prices for oil regulated versus less than cost-recovery domestic prices for gas).

Table 1.5 Production of oil and natural gas in Russia

	1992	1993	1994	1995	1996	1997	1998	1999
Oil	*mbd*	*mbd*	*mbd*	*mbd*	*mbd*	*mbd*	*mbd*	*mbd*
Production	8.02	7.11	6.38	6.16	6.05	6.14	6.09	6.12
Growth rate	–	-11.3	-10.3	-3.4	-1.8	1.5	-0.8	0.5
Natural gas	*bcm*	*bcm*	*bcm*	*bcm*	*bcm*	*bcm*	*bcm*	*Bcm*
Production	641	618.4	607.2	595.4	601.1	571.1	591	590.7
Growth rate	–	-3.5	-1.8	-1.9	1.0	-5.0	3.5	-0.1
	2000	**2001**	**2002**	**2003**	**2004**	**2005**	**2006**	**2007***
Oil	*mbd*	*mbd*	*mbd*	*mbd*	*mbd*	*mbd*	*mbd*	*mbd*
Production	6.49	6.99	7.62	8.46	9.21	9.45	9.64	9.87
Growth rate	6.0	7.7	9.0	11.0	8.9	2.6	2.1	2.4
Natural gas	*bcm*	*bcm*	*bcm*	*bcm*	*Bcm*	*bcm*	*bcm*	*bcm*
Production	584.2	581.5	594.5	620.3	634	640.6	655.5	653
Growth rate	-1.1	-0.5	2.2	4.3	2.2	1.0	2.3	-0.5

* Provisional data for 2007

Sources: Vinhas de Souza (2006) and Troika Dialog.

---

[42] The average growth rate of production during 1999–2004 was close to 9% per year, but fell to around 2.4% in 2005–07.

Box 1.2 The structure of the Russian energy industry

Oil

The Russian oil industry has been reorganised in two steps, starting in 1993. The first phase, completed by 1994, was the transformation of the state-owned concerns into a number of joint stock companies. This was followed in 1995 by the auction of government shares in these companies. This process is still underway, but the trend towards privatisation has almost ground to a halt. The last such auction was the privatisation of the formerly state-owned Russian–Belarusian firm Slavneft in 2002 (although some residual state shareholdings in already privately-owned oil companies have since been sold off, such as the 7.6% stake in Lukoil sold to US ConocoPhilips). Today the oil sector comprises 10 vertically integrated companies that account for almost 95% of Russia's total crude oil production (see Table B1.2). Since the end of 2004, the oil sector has undergone significant and continual restructuring, after Yuganskneftegaz, the main producing asset of Yukos (previously the second-largest privately owned oil company), was sold at an auction and the revenue used to settle tax arrears claimed by the government. Yuganskneftegaz, with a production capacity of 1 mbd, became part of the state-owned company Rosneft, raising the share of fully or partially state-owned firms in total oil production to roughly 34% in 2006 (this figure includes Bashneft, Tatneft and Sibneft, which were acquired by Gazprom in October 2005). The *only* major, direct foreign player in the Russian oil sector is now TNK-BP, a result of the 2003 merger between Tyumen Oil Company (TNK) and British Petroleum (BP).[†]

Table B1.2 Companies' shares in oil and gas production in Russia

	Oil production (mbd)	% in total output	Gas production (bcm)	% in total output
Russia Total	9.7	100.0	655.5	100.0
Lukoil	1.8	18.9	12.0	1.8
Rosneft (+Yuganskneftegaz)*	1.6	17.0	13.7	2.1
TNK–BP	1.5	15.0	8.5	1.3
Surgutneftegaz	1.3	13.7	14.7	2.2
Gazprom/GazpromNeft*	0.9	9.6	550.2	83.9
Tatneft*	0.5	5.2	–	–
Slavneft	0.5	4.9	–	–
Yukos	0.4	4.5	–	–
RussNeft	0.3	3.1	–	–
Bashneft*	0.2	2.5	–	–
NOVATEK	–	–	30.0	4.6
Other producers	0.6	5.7	26.3	4.0

* State-owned or participated.
Sources: Vinhas de Souza (2006) and Troika Dialog.

Box 1.2, cont.

Gas

Unlike the oil sector, the gas industry has never truly departed from the ownership structure inherited from the Soviet period. Prices are regulated, exports are monopolised and the domestic market is dominated by the state-controlled, vertically integrated quasi-monopoly, Gazprom. Gazprom holds nearly one-third of the world's natural gas reserves, produces around 84% of all Russia's natural gas, supplies gas to generate close to 50% of the country's electricity and operates its own natural gas pipeline grid. Gazprom is also Russia's largest individual earner of hard currency and the company's tax payments make up almost 25% of the total federal tax revenues. Oil companies and independent gas producers account for around 16% of total domestic gas production, but about a quarter of this is *flared* (i.e. directly burned into the atmosphere after extraction, as a by-product of oil extraction). This practice largely stems from unprofitable gas processing and sales conditions for these producers compared with Gazprom. In most cases, these other producers have to sell the gas to Gazprom or Gazprom has to provide pipeline access to deliver the gas to non-Gazprom buyers. Through Gazprom, Russia also controls most of the gas supply routes from the Caspian and Central Asian regions to Europe (Kalyuzhnova, 2005) and a large share of their production, under long-term reselling contracts. Nevertheless, despite its size and market power, Gazprom is seriously limited by domestic over-regulation: the company must supply natural gas used to heat and power Russia's domestic market at government-regulated prices set below cost-recovery levels. A timetable for the full deregulation of domestic energy prices by 2011 has recently been announced, however (see next section).

---

† In February 2003, BP purchased a 50% stake in TNK, as well as other assets held by TNK's shareholders, for $7 billion – a figure representing the largest single foreign investment in Russia since the collapse of the Soviet Union. The joint company TNK-BP produced 1.45 mbd in 2006, having lost the rank of second-largest oil producer in Russia to Rosneft in 2005.

That being said, the importance of the other natural resource sectors should not be underestimated, especially given the fact that the contribution of the energy sector to growth in Russia has been declining for years now (Ahrend, 2006). The natural resource sectors[43] indeed *directly*

---

[43] The natural resource sectors include fuel (oil and gas), nonferrous metals and forestry.

contributed around 28% to GDP growth during 2000–06 and the oil industry alone close to 19%.[44] Still, the contribution of the energy sector to industrial growth was actually *negative* until 1998; it seems to have peaked in 2002 and then fallen to 10% by 2006 (according to preliminary estimations, see Figure 1.11).

Figure 1.11 Sector contributions to GDP growth (%)

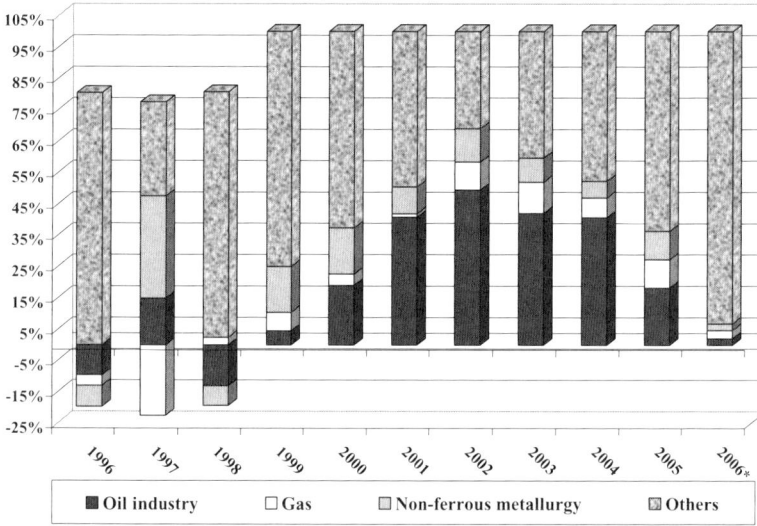

* Preliminary estimations
Sources: Ahrend (2006), Rosstat and author's estimations.

When discussing sectoral contributions to growth in Russia, one must note that Russian official data present a somewhat distorted picture of the importance of the natural resource sectors, because a substantial share of the value added generated by them is reflected not in the accounts of the extraction companies, but in the accounts of their affiliated trading companies. As a result, the export-oriented industries are under-represented in the industrial production figures and the industry as a

[44] On the other hand, as Owen & Robinson (2003) point out, there are likely additional *indirect* contributions of the energy sector to overall growth (through consumption, investment and government revenue) that are not taken into account by this methodology.

whole is under-represented as a share of Russia's GDP, while the trade and services sectors are over-represented.

There have been attempts to correct these distortions. Estimates by the World Bank (2003) using figures for 2000 raise the share of industry in GDP from 27% to 41% and the share of the oil and gas sectors from around 8% to just above 19%, while revising the share of the services sectors downwards from 60% to 46%. The Russian Ministry of Finance produced similar estimates that suggest that the share of the oil and gas sectors in GDP was around 21% in 2000 and around 17% thereafter (given that the growth rates of the energy sector lag considerably behind those of Russia's GDP, this reduction in importance has likely continued). Figure 1.12 shows the structure of industrial value added by sector under the official and adjusted weights. The estimations of sectoral contributions to industrial growth presented in Figure 1.11 above use the corrected weights derived from the World Bank (2003) study.

Figure 1.12 Structure of industrial value added in 2000 (with official data in the top panel and adjusted data from the World Bank in the bottom panel)

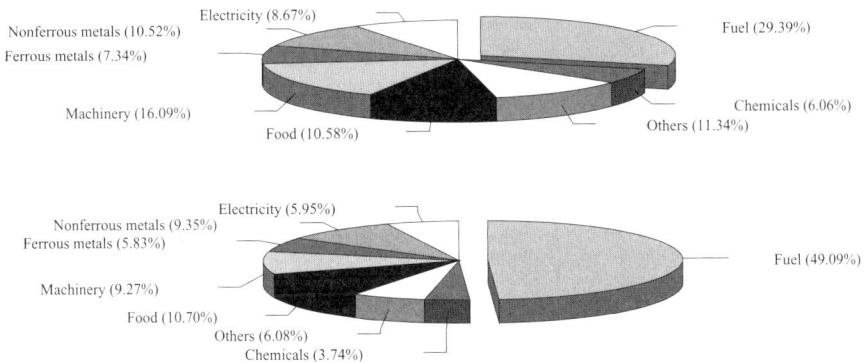

Electricity (8.67%)
Nonferrous metals (10.52%)
Ferrous metals (7.34%)
Fuel (29.39%)
Machinery (16.09%)
Chemicals (6.06%)
Food (10.58%)
Others (11.34%)

Electricity (5.95%)
Nonferrous metals (9.35%)
Ferrous metals (5.83%)
Fuel (49.09%)
Machinery (9.27%)
Food (10.70%)
Others (6.08%)
Chemicals (3.74%)

Sources: Rosstat and World Bank.

Concerning the over 70% of Russian growth that was not *directly* related to natural resources during this period, there has been strong growth in sectors like machine-building and services. Therefore, growth performance in Russia is linked, to a very considerable degree, to the effects of liberalisation reforms in the non-energy sectors of the economy.[45]

The main GDP driver from a demand-side perspective during this period was the increase in *private consumption*, with its GDP share rising by 5% between 2000 and 2006 (see Figure 1.13). This rise was supported by increases in real disposable incomes and the appreciation of the exchange rate. Real wages grew by around 130% during 1999–2004 and were more than 40% above the 1998 levels at the end of this period.

Figure 1.13 Demand-side components of GDP, 1999–2006

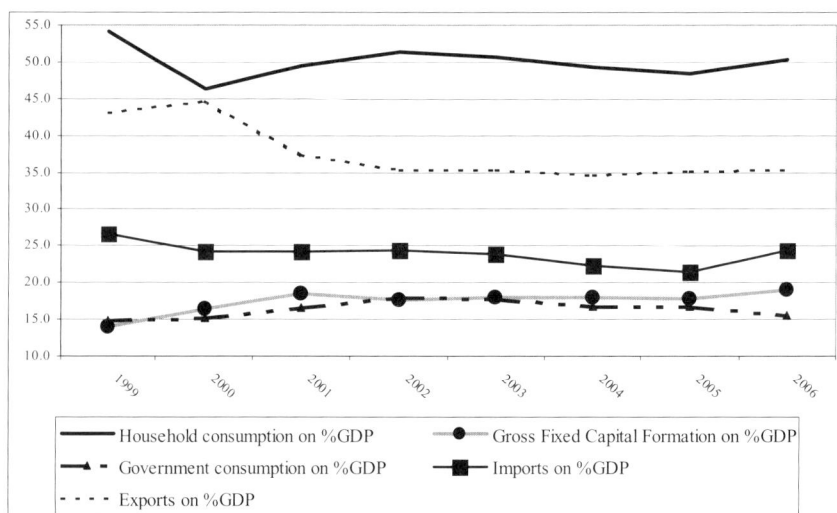

Legend:
— Household consumption on %GDP
—●— Gross Fixed Capital Formation on %GDP
—▲— Government consumption on %GDP
—■— Imports on %GDP
- - - - Exports on %GDP

Source: IMF.

[45] Which of these two elements, oil prices or reforms, has been more important for growth resumption in Russia so far? There is no precise way to assess this, as oil prices and reforms interact in complex ways (one can argue that oil prices hinder reforms – the 'resource curse' argument – but they also provide a source of funds that can enable costly reforms to be undertaken). Nonetheless, estimating a simple, naïve regression of GDP growth rates on oil prices and the EBRD's Transition Indicator for Russia shows that the Transition Indicator variable has a considerably higher (and always positive) coefficient than the one associated with oil prices, which can even have a negative sign (albeit *neither* of the two is always significant). This outcome is robust to the use of the variables in changes or index terms, and to their use in a contemporaneous or lagged format. It is also mostly robust to sample changes (using a sample for either 1989–2006 or 1998–2006).

Therefore, during this period, growth was increasingly *driven* by consumption, but *sustained* by rising export volumes (Owen & Robinson, 2003; Ahrend, 2006). The contribution of *net exports* to growth was small but positive, as export *volume* growth counteracted the upward trend in imports. In 2005, however, this changed. Consumption growth accelerated, supported by fiscal stimulus. This increase supported the expansion of the services sectors, but its impact on the domestically-oriented manufacturing sector was relatively limited. Additionally, a slowdown in the mining sectors was observed, mainly driven by crude extraction. As a result, the contribution of net exports to growth turned negative in 2005.

This slowdown was a consequence of the fall in oil sector investment (even as oil prices rose, capital expenditure by oil companies in Russia fell in real terms during 2004).[46] This investment fall was in turn caused by a deterioration of the business climate, as the footprint of the state in the economy expanded, exemplified by the notorious Yukos case. (When Yukos, previously the largest privately owned oil company in Russia was driven to bankruptcy by claims of alleged back taxes, its assets were sold mostly to state-owned companies and its owners were sent to prison.) A softening of oil prices in late 2006 to early 2007 aggravated this trend.

1.5.3   2006–07: *The beginnings of a new growth cycle?*

2006 and 2007 were further good economic years for Russia, with increases in growth and further cuts in inflation and unemployment. Even so, these years also brought deeper changes, which *may* herald a new Russian growth model:

- Russia has experienced a strong reversal of its traditional capital outflows. Yearly inflows of foreign direct investment (FDI) have reached 3.2% of GDP – a value similar to other major emerging economies.

- Finally, after several years of robust growth, investment in 2006 was the most dynamic demand-side component of GDP. The roughly 22% investment share of GDP is in line with the OECD average.

---

[46] An increase in energy-sector capital expenditure in nominal US dollars was observed in 2004, linked to the Sakhalin I and II Production Sharing Agreement projects. Still, owing to the strong appreciation of the ruble to the US dollar in that year, total oil sector investment in ruble terms declined (Ahrend, 2006).

Moreover, 2007 represents the ninth consecutive year of strong growth in Russia, supported by domestic demand – especially investment – and increasing energy prices. In 2006, real GDP growth was 7.4%, up from 6.4% in 2005. As indicated above, the Rosstat estimate for 2007 growth is 8.1%, with nominal Russian GDP expected to reach close to $1.35 trillion by end-2007 (or larger than the size of the Spanish GDP). The key factors behind this higher-than-expected growth are

1)   an acceleration of investment spending, supported by a continuation of the very significant increase of net capital inflows observed since full capital account liberalisation in mid-2006;

2)   a rebound in oil prices, after the softening observed in late 2006/early 2007; and

3)   the increase in public spending connected with the 2007–08 electoral cycle.

On the demand side, the most notable development in 2006–07 has been the take-off of investment (with gross capital formation having soared by almost 21% year-on-year (yoy) in 2007, compared with 17.5% in 2006).[47] Government spending has also accelerated. At the same time, overall consumption growth, still the main driver of growth, has decelerated, while net exports have amplified their negative contribution to growth (-14.3% in 2006).

---

[47] Russia has been able to achieve and sustain the high growth rates of the past decade despite comparatively low investment and significantly lower FDI inflows per capita (on this point, see the FDI discussion in section 2.3), even when compared with most other CIS economies. During 2001–04, investment as a share of GDP reached around 18%, which is significantly below the level of other fast-growing emerging economies and well below the OECD average of around 22%. Growth has been possible partially because of the existence of considerably unused installed capacity, which by late 2006 had fallen to 15%. On the other hand, it must be noted that in early transition economies investment is usually *not significant for growth*. This is because transition economies' initial growth is not analogous to the normal long-term equilibrium growth path. As Vinhas de Souza & Havrylyshyn (2006) point out, the dynamics in this period were not a matter of moving the economy to a higher production possibility frontier (PPF) through the expansion of factor inputs or technological change, but rather a matter of correcting the large inefficiencies of the communist period, moving from within the scope of the PPF *to* the outer edge of the PPF, and shifting resource allocation *along* the PPF to an internationally comparative advantage position.

Reflecting these developments, industrial production growth in 2006 was below 4%, but grew rapidly in 2007, reaching 7.9% by the end of the year. This performance of the construction and trade sectors was also strong (with yoy growth rates of, respectively, 16.4% and 12%), with the extraction of mineral resources (oil and gas) showing a mere 0.3% increase yoy (after 1.6% in 2006).

This continued, robust growth performance has led to a further significant fall in unemployment, which reached 6.1% in December 2007 (according to the International Labour Organisation methodology), compared with 6.9% at the end of 2006. Major metropolitan areas (Moscow and St Petersburg) effectively face labour shortages in many sectors. Correspondingly, real disposable income has grown by up to 14% yoy in 2007.

The 2007 trade surplus fell below 10% of GDP, from 14% in 2006. This reduction reflects the low growth of export volumes and the continued growth of import volumes at substantially higher rates than those of exports. Similarly, the current account surplus declined from almost 10% of GDP in 2006 to below 6% in 2007.

An implication of this reduction in the current account surplus is the consequent decline of the excess liquidity that has been hampering monetary policy (see section 2.2.2). If this trend persists, the currently negative, real short-term interest rates may turn positive, affecting both households and firms, and enabling the CBR to become a liquidity provider in the interbank market (as it did during the financial turbulence of August 2007, also discussed below).

For this to happen, however, *the capital account should not fully compensate the reduction in the current account balance*. In another development, FDI flowing into Russia – an area in which the country has traditionally underperformed – more than doubled between 2005 and 2006, from $14.6 billion to $31 billion. FDI yearly inflows as a share of GDP stand at over 3.2% (up from 2% in 2005), a level very similar to other major emerging markets such as China. Total net private-sector capital inflows reached $41.6 billion, up from $1.1 billion in 2005, reversing the persistent *net capital outflows* since 1994. This positive performance seems to have continued during 2007, as discussed in the next chapter.

What can one conclude from this chapter? After the troubled 1990s, Russia has so far effectively used the opportunity provided by high oil prices after 1999. When compared with similarly large emerging markets (some of which are also countries exporting substantial natural resources), Russia has the second-best 1999–2006 growth performance, with an average growth rate of 6.7% (just below China's performance of 9.2%, which, by any historical yardstick, is truly exceptional). Figure 1.14 shows that Russia comfortably beats the 5.4% average of the comparator group of BRIC countries (Brazil, Russia, India and China) plus Saudi Arabia.[48]

Figure 1.14 Growth in large emerging markets, 1999–2006 (%)

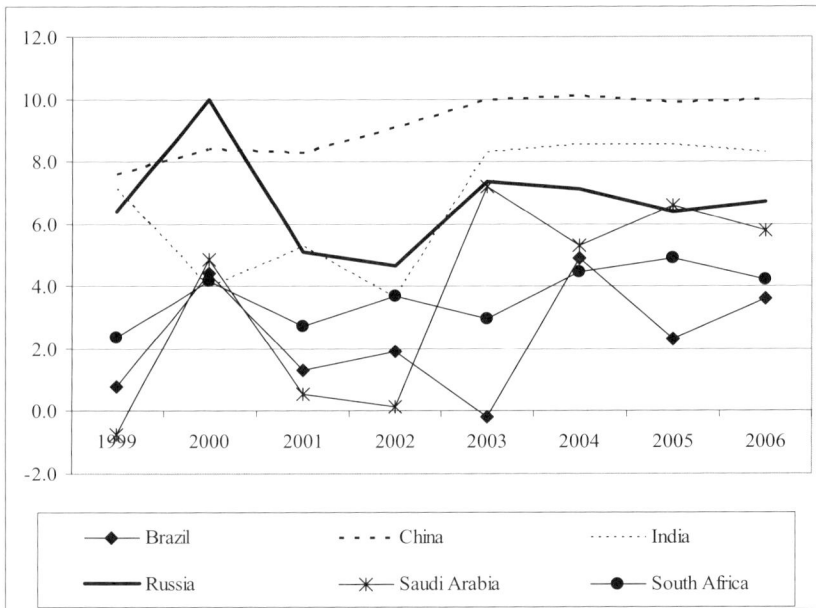

Source: IMF.

---

[48] Beck, Kamps & Mileva (2007) estimate the current (i.e. without any additional growth-enhancing structural reform) long-term growth potential of Russia to be within the robust 4-6% interval.

As pointed out above, Russia could be on the verge of switching to a more sustainable growth model, driven by higher domestic investment and FDI inflows.[49] To take full advantage of this situation, making growth truly sustainable in the long run, the *necessary macroeconomic frameworks and structural reforms* have to be in place. These are dealt with in the next chapters.

---

[49] One could also point out that the high endowment of human capital in Russia is potentially supportive of such an economic diversification strategy. The Russian population is highly educated: secondary enrolment in 2004 was 93%, while tertiary enrolment was 65%. This rate is very similar to high-income countries and far above the rate in BRIC countries, such as China (15%). On the other hand, indicators of spending on education remain below the BRIC average. Russia also produces a much greater share of graduates in science and engineering subjects than higher-income countries. The number of persons in R&D per million of population is comparable to Germany and much higher than in the BRICs: in 2005, Russia had almost 1 million persons engaged in R&D activities. This figure is similar to China's, and about half of the EU-25 figure.

2. RUSSIA UNDER PUTIN:
   THE INCOMPLETE REFORM AGENDA

As indicated at the beginning of this book, economic reform has to be placed within the political constraints of a particular situation. For Russia in the late 1990s, this meant the change between the first and second Presidents of the Russian Federation, from Boris Yeltsin to Vladimir Putin. This chapter describes the reforms undertaken during the two terms of Vladimir Putin's Presidency, and the remaining main reform challenges.

2.1 Russia under Vladimir Putin

2.1.1 Filling the reform vacuum

After a bruising 1996 re-election campaign (which left him beholden to the oligarch class), the traumatic 1998 crisis and the muddled policy response to it,[50] not to mention his clearly worsening health, President Yeltsin was a diminished political figure, no longer capable of spearheading reform. The search for his successor began.

On 9 August 1999 – less than a year after the 1998 crisis – Vladimir Vladimirovich Putin, a former KGB/FSB officer with long international experience (he had served for many years in the former East Germany) and who had participated in one of the first reformist regional governments in his native St Petersburg, was appointed Prime Minister by Boris Yeltsin. He replaced Sergei Stepashin. Mr Yeltsin also announced that he wished to see Vladimir Putin as his successor.

---

[50] The policy response was exemplified by the inconsistent Maslyukov plan, named after First Deputy Prime Minister Yuri Maslyukov, which largely relied on proposed fiscal easing as a way to cushion the crisis.

On 31 December 1999, Boris Yeltsin resigned, three months before the end of his term. Vladimir Putin was appointed acting President of the Russian Federation.[51] Snap presidential elections were held on 26 March 2000, which Mr Putin duly won. (On 14 March 2004, he would be re-elected for a second term, with 71% of the vote.)

Vladimir Putin moved fast to fill the reform vacuum left by the final years of the Yeltsin administration. By mid-2000, a comprehensive reform plan that would essentially map out economic reform in Russia for the next eight years had already been designed and approved. This was the Gref plan (see Box 2.1). Most of its economic policy items have been effectively implemented – even if partially – while the social policy items have lagged behind (although some of the 2007 pre-election four National Priority Projects, in education, health, housing and agriculture can actually be traced back to the Gref plan).

It is perhaps more discerning to see President Putin's government not so much as a non-reforming one, as is frequently portrayed, but as an uneasy conjunction of a solidly reforming 'quartet' of institutions – the Ministry of Finance, the Ministry for Economic Development and Trade (MEDT), the CBR and the recently created Federal Service for Financial Markets – that share political space with a nationalist and statist circle, the so-called *siloviki*.[52] These two circles frequently run inconsistent and parallel economic policies, and their relative influence has varied in accordance with the economic cycle (and the related strength of oil prices). In any case, this reformist group of institutions has been quite effective in pushing for liberalising reforms. This is partly owing to their *permanence*, as essentially the same group of people has run these institutions from the beginning of Vladimir Putin's government, and most of them have worked with Mr Putin since his initial experience in government in St Petersburg.[53] In

[51] In his first decree on that day, Mr Putin granted Boris Yeltsin and his family legal immunity from prosecution in Russia.

[52] *Siloviki* refers to former (or, in some cases, still active) members from the security services (KGB/FSB) and the military.

[53] The cabinet reform of September 2007 elevated Finance Minister Alexei Kudrin to Deputy Prime Minister and replaced MEDT Minister German Gref (who became Chairman of Sberbank) by another reformer, Elvira Nabiullina (herself a co-author of the Gref plan). As shown in the previous chapter, the degree of personnel continuity within the Russian government is considerably deeper than one realises at first sight.

December 2007, President Putin anointed (as did Boris Yeltsin) his successor, Dmitry Anatolyevich Medvedev, who is a member of his St Petersburg circle and currently First Deputy Prime Minister of Russia, responsible for the implementation of the National Priority Projects along with being Chairman of Gazprom. He was duly elected in March 2008, and appointed Putin as his Prime Minister.

Box 2.1 President Putin as an economic reformer: The Gref plan

In July 2000, the Russian government published the "Social & Economic Policy Programme 2000–2010". (It is also known as the Gref plan, after German Gref, the Minister for Economic Development and Trade and head of the think tank Centre for Strategic Research, who authored most of the plan in conjunction with the Bureau of Economic Analysis, a think tank linked to the Ministry of Finance.) The key measures in this plan are summarised below.

Social policy. Objectives: i) to improve the protection of socially vulnerable households; ii) to ensure universal accessibility to and an acceptable quality of basic social benefits, especially for health care and education; iii) to enable working-age individuals to enjoy higher consumption levels based on their own income; and iv) to attract household and enterprise funds to help finance social sector institutions. Priority social policy measures by *sector* include:

- an increase of public spending on education and an improvement of the transparency of financial flows in the education sector;
- the restructure of small rural schools and the establishment of federal and regional educational standards;
- the provision of full financing to fulfil state guarantees for the delivery of free health care to the public, and an expansion of the range of organisational and legal forms of health care institutions;
- the reform of labour legislation, including the Labour Code, with a view to increasing labour mobility and improving the balance of interests between workers, employers and the state. Termination procedures are to be simplified. The financing of unemployment benefits are to be transferred to the federal budget. Increases in the minimum wage are to be continued; and
- the reform of social assistance on the principle of providing mostly targeted assistance, only to households whose consumption is below the subsistence level. Social category-based federal benefits are to be eliminated except for groups like war veterans and invalids, and such benefits transformed into cash payments. Real pensions are to rise while ensuring the financial sustainability of the system. A funded pillar is to be set up in the pension system. Pensions are to be indexed to a combination of wages and prices. Consideration is to be given to the need for gradual adjustment of the pension age. Subsidies are to be cut and housing benefits increasingly targeted.

Box 2.1, cont.

Economic policy. Objectives: i) to establish legislative principles promoting a favourable business and investment climate; ii) to reduce the tax burden substantially while ensuring medium-term financial stability; and iii) to stimulate progressive structural changes in the economy, reform the infrastructure monopolies, develop the financial infrastructure and foster the development of Russia's technical and research potential.

Priority economic policy measures by *sector* include

- an improvement in the protection of property rights, including laws to protect shareholder and creditor rights, and intellectual property rights. Equal competition conditions are to be created, including the elimination of most direct and indirect subsidies to inefficient companies. Excessive state interference in business is to be reduced, with simplified registration and licensing procedures and reductions in the numbers of inspection and monitoring bodies. International Accounting Standards are to be introduced and financial disclosure requirements vigorously enforced;

- banking system reform, including legal amendments to facilitate the liquidation of unviable banks, and the development of deposit insurance. With respect to capital market expansion, the range of available financial instruments is to be extended, tax incentives are to be introduced to encourage the growth of non-government pension funds and investment in Russian securities, and capital market regulation is to be improved. Mortgage markets are to be developed. The emergence of national insurance companies is to be encouraged through tax incentives, legislation on mandatory insurance and the development of a public regulation and supervisory system;

- tax reform, with reductions to the average customs duty rates and their diversity (in concordance with accession negotiations with the World Trade Organisation), the elimination of customs privileges and the introduction of new customs administration technologies. Fiscal policy objectives include the elimination of non-funded mandates, an inventory of public assets and liabilities, the evaluation of public expenditure effectiveness and steps to ensure an appropriate, transparent allocation of expenditure responsibility and resource availability to different levels of government. Inflation is to be reduced to low levels by targeting money supply growth, the range of available monetary policy instruments is to be extended and the payments system is to be modernised;

Box 2.1, cont.

- the privatisation of a significant number of state-owned enterprises and improvements to state property management. State funding is to be provided for R&D and venture investment. The military-industrial complex is to be restructured to increase efficiency, reduce energy intensity and encourage conversion to civilian use. Competitive agricultural product markets are to be established; and

- reform of the infrastructure monopolies, including restructuring to separate naturally monopolistic and potentially competitive activities, improvements in the network access for independent gas producers and rail operators, the de-monopolisation of electricity generation and telecoms, significant reductions in the lists of customers whose energy supply may not be cut off and reductions in cross-subsidies between categories of customers. Energy efficiency is to be encouraged, the taxation of the fuel and energy sector is to be improved and the legislation on Production Sharing Agreements is to be developed.

Source: IMF.

2.1.2   Is Russia such a poor reformer?

As exemplified in the previous chapter concerning growth, when evaluating Russia's overall performance in economic reform, it is essential to use adequate benchmarks. The usual comparison with other former centrally planned economies in Central Europe is not fully correct. In those economies, the process of integration into the EU implied *binding* structural reforms imposed by the powerful external anchor of the EU accession process.[54] For the CIS, no such strong external anchor exists. Therefore, Russia's reform process should be compared with clusters of countries that do not benefit from such external constraints.

Using a traditional index of reform – the transition indicator[55] of the European Bank for Reconstruction and Development (EBRD) – to compare Russia with clusters of other transition countries reveals several things (see Figure 2.1).

---

[54] This statement is no way implies the questioning of the overall desirability of external anchors for reform.

[55] For a description of the indicator, see EBRD (several issues).

Figure 2.1 EBRD transition indicators for Russia and regional groups

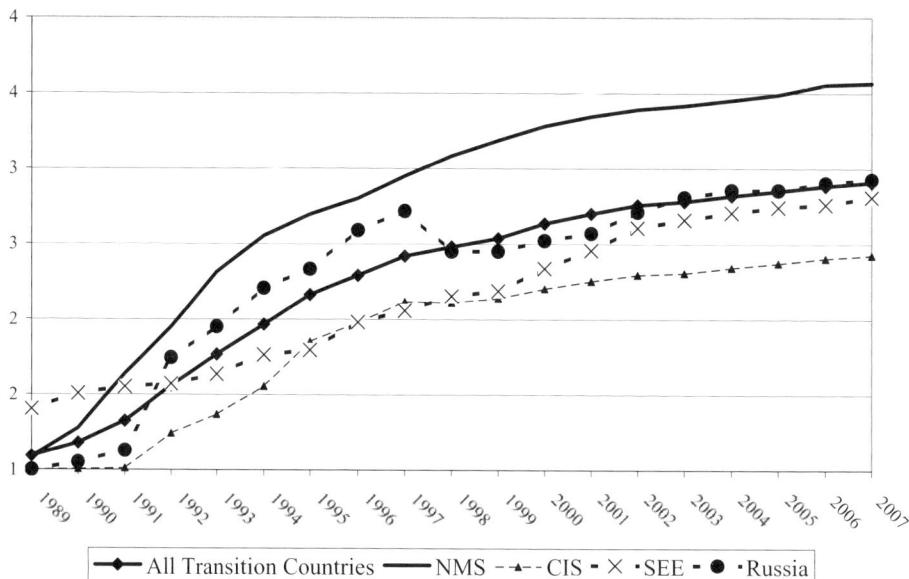

Source: EBRD.

First, Russia outperforms the CIS average and with increasing distance (in other words, Russia is reforming faster than the CIS (non-GDP weighted) average, which includes some very slow reformers). Second, Russia is very close to the average of the Balkans, which includes two EU candidate countries, Croatia and the former Yugoslav Republic of Macedonia (which together raise the average reform performance of the Balkan countries). Third, progress in structural reform in Russia as measured by the transition indicator resumed in 2006 after a hiatus in 2004–05.[56] Finally, the new EU member states from Eastern Europe clearly outperform all the other groupings, as one should expect. It is possible to

---

[56] This hiatus was linked to an expansion of the role of the state in the economy, as demonstrated by the takeover of Yukos. That move led to a reduction of the private sector share in GDP from 70% to 65% between 2004 and 2005. In 2006, the share stabilised at 65%. This figure still puts Russia above the CIS average of 56%, and at the same level of other large CIS economies such as Kazakhstan and Ukraine, and just above the south-eastern European and overall transition economy average of 64% (but considerably below the new member state average of 73%).

identify the specific reform areas in which Russia underperforms (not shown in Figure 2.1 above – see EBRD, several issues): these are competition policy, corporate governance and enterprise restructuring (i.e. microeconomic and structural areas, arguably more difficult to reform; conversely, Russia performs better on more traditional *macro* areas of reform).

Using other transition country indicators, Russia also shows a mixed performance in improving its business environment (equally a microeconomic/structural concern). For instance, according to the results of the EBRD–World Bank Business Environment and Enterprise Performance Survey (BEEPS), between 2002 and 2005, private sector perceptions of the level of effectiveness of the judiciary, the extent of corruption and labour regulation worsened – substantially in the case of corruption. At the same time, the perception of customs and trade regulations, business licensing and permits, and tax administration improved. Significantly, Russia is below the CIS average in *all* these categories, but tellingly its performance is strikingly similar to the other resource-rich CIS economies, Azerbaijan and Kazakhstan.

Going beyond the set of transition economies, how does Russia compare with other large emerging markets? This question has particular relevance given that, for instance, when a foreign investor is evaluating the decision to engage in an FDI operation in Russia, his or her comparator country will not necessarily be Estonia, Slovenia or even Poland, but rather other resource/endowment-rich BRIC giants like Brazil, China or India.

One can do that sort of comparison using the global World Bank survey of business regulations and their enforcement, entitled *Doing Business 2008* (which refers to 2007 data). There, Russia ranks 106th out of 178 countries, above countries such as Brazil and India but behind China (this is a relative deterioration compared with its 2006 ranking of 96th out of 175 countries, although the changes in the index methodology and in the sample of countries make inter-year comparisons rather difficult). Russia is close to the average rank of the CIS countries (this average is significantly influenced by one country, Georgia, which is now classified as one of the 20 easiest places in the world to do business), and above EU-leaning countries like Ukraine (see Figure 2.2). The areas in which Russia performs worst when compared with the CIS average are "licensing requirements", "dealing with workers" (where its stands at roughly the EU and OECD averages) and "trading across borders" (export and import costs are comparatively high in Russia, which is partially related to the sheer size of the country). On the other hand, it ranks *above* the OECD and the EU on items like "enforcing contracts" (19th),[57] "registering property" (45th) and "starting a business" (50th).

Figure 2.2 Doing Business 2008 rankings for Russia and others

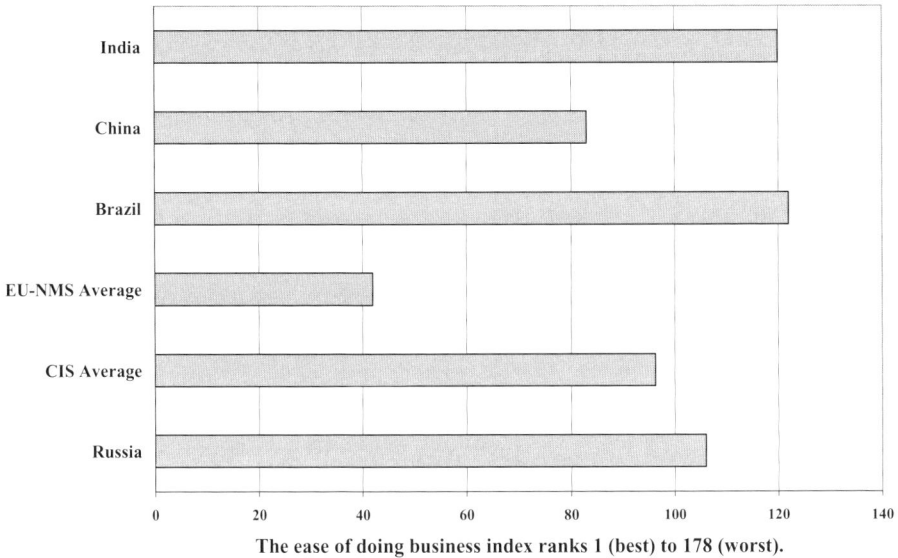

The ease of doing business index ranks 1 (best) to 178 (worst).

Source: World Bank.

Another set of global World Bank statistics, its Governance Indicators, presents a consistent picture with the results of the *Doing Business* survey, but not necessarily with the BEEPS. According to these indicators, between 2002 and 2004 an improvement was observed in "government effectiveness", "rule of law" and "control of corruption", whereas "regulatory quality" and "voice and accountability" worsened. Here also, the quality of Russia's business environment compares relatively favourably with that of the other major emerging economies.

When one uses the World Economic Forum's *Global Competitiveness Report 2007*, a similar global benchmarking index, Russia ranks 58th out of 131 countries – the highest rank of all CIS countries covered and ahead of

---

[57] This ranking admittedly may come as a surprise to BP, Shell or Yukos investors.

three EU member states and Brazil, but below China and India. Russia's main weaknesses here are "institutions" (it fares close to the bottom in 'usual suspect' categories like protection of minority shareholders and property rights) and in "goods market efficiency" (where it ranks much lower on some items related to FDI).

The overall conclusion from this section is that Russia, albeit far from being a model reformer, does not necessarily do badly when compared with adequate benchmarks. Furthermore, the perception of an overall slowdown in reforms is not necessarily accurate.[58]

This observation, of course, does not mean that further reforms are not necessary (especially in more microeconomic and structural areas) – *far from it*. The following sections look at *specific* components of the macroeconomic framework and the various sets of structural policies of the Russian Federation.

2.2 Fiscal and monetary institutions and the financial system

2.2.1 *Recent fiscal performance and fiscal institutions*

Russia's headline fiscal position has substantially improved since 1998, in line with the increase in energy prices. A prudent fiscal policy has arguably been the *single most important factor in the economic recovery since 1998.*

The federal budget swung from a deficit of almost 6% of GDP to a surplus of 7.4% in 2006 (see Figure 1.8 above). The growth of energy-related revenues was fundamental to this outcome: in 2000, the combined share of oil and gas revenues amounted to 22% of total federal budget revenues (or 3.4% of GDP), but this share climbed to 50% (or nearly 12% of GDP) in 2006. The increase reflects both higher energy prices and significant rises in oil taxation.[59] Also important for Russia's fiscal

---

[58] In any case, it is also true that Russia, having started at roughly the same level as that of Eastern Europe, is now clearly behind the new EU member states in terms of reforms.

[59] Partially reflecting the power of the oligarch class in influencing government policy in Russia, mineral export taxes were actually abolished in 1996, but reintroduced in 1999. In 2002, a new tax on minerals production (equivalent to a royalty) was introduced as part of a further tax reform for the oil sector. It replaced a number of earlier taxes related to oil production and simplified the overall tax system. This last reform established a maximum rate for the oil export tax linked to

sustainability was the fiscal reform undertaken in 2001, which unified and lowered income tax brackets. Additionally, the re-centralisation of revenue at the federal level under President Putin, reversing the frequently ad hoc arrangements with the regions stemming from the Yeltsin period, had a major role in this process.

Fiscal indicators other than the headline deficit/surplus, however, show a less rosy picture. Among those, the *constant oil price fiscal balance*[60] is used to evaluate how fiscal policy responds to the oil price cycle. The *non-oil fiscal balance*[61] is used to evaluate how the fiscal position is affected by the inflow of oil revenues and how actual fiscal policy differs from the 'optimal' fiscal policy in the presence of non-renewable resources such as oil and gas. The constant oil price fiscal balance in Russia, using a $20 benchmark, deteriorated between 2001 and 2003, but showed a modest improvement in 2004, before worsening substantially again in 2005 and 2006. Similarly, the non-oil federal government fiscal balance reached a deficit of -3.8% of GDP in 2006; it is forecast to reach -4.3% in 2007 (IMF estimates).[62]

---

the world oil price. The tax regime for the oil sector underwent further significant changes in 2004, leading to an added increase in the tax burden on the sector, particularly on oil exports. The new, more progressive scale of taxation seeks to withdraw the 'additional profits' from oil exporters when world oil prices are high, while at the same time lightening the overall tax burden.

[60] The *constant oil price fiscal balance* takes as a benchmark the long-term oil price level. The implicit assumption underlying it is that the price of oil tends to revert to this long-term benchmark, so an 'optimal' fiscal policy should aim at balancing the fiscal position with oil revenues at this long-term level.

[61] In order to maximise welfare over the long term, a country endowed with a given amount of non-renewable resources should smooth consumption and non-renewable resource taxation; for instance, revenues coming from oil and gas should first be partly accumulated in an oil investment fund and used in principle only *after* the depletion of the non-renewable resources (see IMF, various years). The implication of such a policy is that the *non-oil primary balance should be constant over time*, but the *level* of the optimal primary balance is not predetermined, as it depends on many variables (the amount of non-renewable resources, the social discount rate, etc.).

[62] This figure does not include the increase in revenue after the elimination of the offshore oil arrangement with Belarus, which is expected to increase Russian fiscal revenues by at least $1 billion (European Commission, 2007).

Helped by high growth, federal spending remained below 15% of GDP in both 2004 and 2005 despite significant nominal increases.[63] Nevertheless, as Russia is a federal nation,[64] the regional dimension has to be included: the unified *regional* budgets add another 14% to the previous figures – in other words, they are as large as the federal budget itself. Together with off-budget social funds, the regional budgets bring the consolidated government expenditures in Russia to more than 30% of GDP (see Table 2.1).

Furthermore, unlike the federal government, Russian regions posted only a marginal surplus in 2004 and 2005 (0.3-0.2% of GDP), largely because regional budgets have only been able to benefit indirectly from higher energy prices, through an increase in profit tax revenues (which reached close to 40% of the total regional budget tax revenues in 2005, before federal transfers). Federal transfers have also fallen, as the Russian 'fiscal federalism' arrangement seems to be evolving away from the present equalisation schemes towards a regional policy based on a 'differentiation' approach (with the application of regional fiscal rules that reward, among other things, budgetary performance).

In any case, the 2006 federal budget surplus (Russia has had budget surpluses since 2000) was roughly at the same level as in 2005, despite the significant rise in expenditure, and far above the government-projected forecast in the 2006 budget of 3.2% (this forecast was based on a conservative oil price assumption of $40 per barrel in the 2006 budget).

Since 2006, Russia has embarked on a strong fiscal expansion programme, linked to the 2007–08 election cycle.[65] Non-interest expenditures in the 2007 budget are set to increase by around 1% of GDP at the federal level. This increase follows a previous one during 2006. Most of this increase (around 0.7% of GDP) is linked to the pre-electoral National

---

[63] This total includes the 2005 cut in the transfers from the unified social tax to the Russian pension fund; non-interest expenditure excluding the unified social tax actually *rose* by almost 2% of GDP in 2005.

[64] Russia has 84 administrative units, which include autonomous and ethnic republics, *oblasts, krais, okrugs* and the cities of Moscow and St Petersburg (not to mention over 24,000 municipalities).

[65] The parliamentary elections were held in December 2007, which were comfortably won by the ruling party, United Russia, and the presidential elections in March 2008, with Dmitry Medvedev receiving over 70% of the vote.

Priority Projects in the areas of agriculture, education, health and housing. The budget surplus fell to 5.5% of GDP in 2007 (in August 2007, it was still at 7.1% of GDP). Russia's twin surpluses (in the fiscal and external accounts) have also enabled the country to reduce its gross public debt to a massive extent (i.e. including both external and domestic debt), which was halved between 2005 and 2006 (from 16.4% of GDP to 8.6%).

Table 2.1 Summary of operations of the enlarged government, 2000–05 (% of GDP)

	2000	2001	2002	2003	2004	2005	2006
General government							
Overall balance	3.1	2.7	0.7	1.5	4.9	8.1	7.4
Primary balance	7.4	5.4	2.8	3.2	6.3	9.2	8.1
Revenues	36.8	37.3	37.7	36.3	36.8	40.0	41.0
Expenditures	33.7	34.6	37.0	34.9	31.9	31.9	32.8
Federal government							
Overall balance	0.8	2.7	1.3	1.7	4.3	7.5	7.4
Primary balance	5.2	5.4	3.4	3.4	5.5	8.4	–
Revenues	15.4	17.8	17.2	16.8	17.6	22.5	23.2
Expenditures	14.6	15.1	15.9	15.1	13.3	15.0	15.8
Local government							
Overall balance	0.8	-0.2	-0.5	-0.4	0.2	0.3	–
Revenues	15.4	15.0	15.2	14.6	14.2	13.9	–
incl. transfers	1.7	2.7	2.7	2.9	2.4	2.4	–
Expenditures	14.6	15.2	15.7	15.0	14.0	13.6	–
*Extra-budgetary funds**							
Overall balance	1.4	0.2	-0.2	0.1	0.4	0.4	–
Revenues	8.3	8.0	8.8	8.6	8.1	8.3	–
incl. transfers	0.6	0.7	0.8	0.7	0.7	2.3	–
Expenditures	6.8	7.7	9.0	8.4	7.7	8.0	–

* Extra-budgetary funds refer to pensions, employment, social insurance and medical insurance funds.

Sources: IMF Article IV consultation documents (2006), Rosstat, Troika Dialog and DB Research.

At his 26 April 2007 (and presumably last) Annual Address to the State Duma, President Putin unveiled a package of additional pre-electoral spending estimated at RUB 650 billion, implying (if fully executed) further fiscal expenditures worth around 2% of GDP, spread over 2007–09. This package includes social measures (housing and pensions), the capitalisation of a new Russian Development Bank and the creation of off-budget innovation and economic diversification funds (the largest of which is the Nanotechnology Corporation).[66] Later in 2007, another fiscal package worth RUB 300 billion was announced to support the 2014 Winter Olympics in Sochi (effectively a regional development programme for the whole region, Krasnodar Krai).

The fiscal framework has been further strengthened by decisions taken in April 2007.[67] The Russian Oil Stabilisation Fund (StabFund), having been established in 2003 and remained the main fiscal restraint framework in Russia, was divided in February 2008 into a fiscal stabilisation and an investment component. The fiscal stabilisation part will perform the current StabFund functions (i.e. to shelter fiscal policy from swings in oil prices) and will be fixed at 10% of GDP, while the investment component is *expected* to have some functions akin to a sovereign wealth

---

[66] The capitalisation funds of the development institutions where duly transferred in December 2007, in the usual Russian end-of-year dash to spend budgetary allocations. This particular operation also helped to increase the liquidity of the Russian banking system, in the wake of the summer 2007 episode of financial instability.

[67] Revenues used to accrue to the Russian Oil Stabilisation Fund (or StabFund) from oil exports and production taxes when prices rose above $20 per barrel, but the threshold was raised to $27 after January 2006, and was replaced in February 2008 by fixed tranfers. The StabFund also experienced other significant changes during 2006: its assets were converted from rubles into hard currencies (at the end of 2006, it was composed of $39.4 billion, €30.8 billion and £4.6 billion) and some of its assets can now be invested in triple-A bonds from OECD countries. To give an example of the possible pay-off from such a diversified investment strategy, simulations by the author show the StabFund growing from the current 11% of GDP to almost 18% in 2030, in a low return scenario (using the long-term returns of US Treasuries as a benchmark), and to almost *200%* of GDP in the high return scenario (using the average long-term price premium of stocks over Treasuries). As a comparison, the Norway Oil Fund, which has a similar investment strategy, reached 90% of GDP in 2006.

fund.[68] The StabFund had reached almost $150 billion in accumulated assets by late December 2007 (worth over 11% of GDP).

A medium-term expenditure framework was also formally introduced by the April 2007 reforms (albeit through a simple change in the budget code law, making it a somewhat weaker sort of 'fiscal rule'). This three-year budgetary framework additionally encompasses separate oil and non-oil budgetary systems (to be phased in progressively). These changes include a cap on the transfers from the oil to the non-oil budget, and a limit for the non-oil deficit (see Box 2.2). Moreover, in a gradual move towards performance budgeting, the government has decided to start including performance indicators that will cover an estimated 70% of the expenditure in the federal budget. This last change is especially relevant given the traditionally low effectiveness of public spending in Russia, which is even more worrying given the ongoing election-related fiscal expansion.

This strengthening of the fiscal framework can be seen as an indication that the policy (and political) debate within the Russian government about a more 'liberal' use of the revenues from the energy sector has been won by the fiscally conservative Ministry of Finance, against the more spendthrift MEDT. (This is also reflected in the September 2007 promotion of Finance Minister Alexei Kudrin to Deputy Prime Minister.)

In any case, the 2006 general government budget would still have been balanced at an oil price of $32 per barrel. Despite further fiscal relaxation in 2007, it would be balanced at a price of $40 per barrel (or roughly 40% of the oil price in late December 2007). This suggests that Russia currently taxes and saves a large proportion of its terms-of-trade gains, even under relatively conservative oil price assumptions. Consequently, there might still be scope for fiscal stimuli (through increased spending or tax cuts) in the medium term.

---

[68] In 2005, Russia introduced a separate investment fund, which was managed by the MEDT, but was transferred to the Ministry for Regional Development in the September 2007 cabinet reshuffle. This investment fund has relatively small amounts allocated to it (around $2 billion) and will only consider co-financing projects led by private investment in certain specific priority areas, including infrastructure (in this sense, it is similar to a fund for the co-financing of public–private partnerships, PPPs).

Box 2.2 Changes in the fiscal framework in 2007

Starting from 2008, all Russian budget revenues will be divided into 'oil' and 'non-oil' budgets. Oil revenues will include not only the mineral extraction tax and export duties on crude oil (the taxes that currently generate the StabFund revenues) but also tax proceeds related to oil products and, crucially, natural gas. The transfers from the oil to the non-oil budget will be capped (at 3.7% of GDP, a limit to be reached by 2011), while a binding limit for the non-oil budget deficit will be introduced (set at 4.7% of GDP by 2011).

From 1 February 2008 onwards, the StabFund was divided into a reserve fund, akin to the current StabFund and a 'fund for future generations' (also known as the 'welfare fund'). The former will be fixed at 10% of GDP, and funds in excess of this amount will be transferred to the latter. According to President Putin's April 2007 address to the State Duma, the welfare fund (the assets of which are expected to be invested using a more activist approach than those of the StabFund) are also to be used to finance any shortfall in the pensions system. In addition, the welfare fund is to provide resources for projects to be financed by 'development institutions' such as the 'venture fund' and the Development Bank. The precise nature of the potential uses and the investment rules for the future welfare fund are still under discussion.

The assumption described above that funds from natural resources should be accumulated in a fund until the non-renewable resource is exhausted only holds if a country *does not* start with a less than optimal level of capital stock, if there are *no* positive externalities of public spending on productivity and if *no* intergenerational equity considerations are taken into account. It is arguable whether either of these conditions applies in Russia, and thus there may be a stronger rationale for the *current* usage of oil/gas revenues, for instance on infrastructure projects.

2.2.2 The monetary and exchange-rate policy frameworks and the financial system

Russia has experienced a somewhat slow disinflation process. Until 2006, inflation was stubbornly stuck at the low double-digit levels for several years (see Figure 1.5 in section 1.4.2 above). In 2006, however, CPI inflation fell below two digits, reaching 9%[69] (before jumping back to 11.9% in 2007).

---

[69] This inflation rate is below the CIS and African 2006 averages (9.6% and 9.9%, respectively) and very close to the fuel exporters' average inflation (8.6%) in 2006.

Equally, for the first time, the CBR attained the inflation target it had set at the beginning of 2006 (for the targets in previous years, see Table 2.2). The CBR also undershot its own REER appreciation target, which reached 7.7% in 2006 (against a target of 9%, and compared with the 10% appreciation observed in 2005). Real exchange rate appreciation had brought the ruble significantly above its 1998 level by 2006 (see Figure 1.6 in section 1.4.3).

Table 2.2 Stated objectives and targets of the CBR

1999	2000	2001	2002	2003	2004
M2 aggregate growth rates as an intermediate target: 18-26% growth	M2 aggregate growth rates as an intermediate target: 21-25% growth	M2 aggregate growth rates as an intermediate target: 27-34% growth	M2 aggregate growth rates as an intermediate target: 22-28% growth	M2 aggregate growth rates as an intermediate target: 20-26% growth	M2 aggregate growth rates as an intermediate target: 19-25% growth
Reduction of the inflation rate to 30%	Reduction of the inflation rate to 18%	Reduction of the inflation rate to 12-14% a year	Reduction of inflation to 12-14% a year range (*core inflation concept introduced*)	Reduction of inflation to 10-12% (core inflation should be kept within the 8.0-8.5% range)	Reduction of inflation to 8-10% (or 7-8% core inflation), to 6.5-8.5% in 2005 and to 5.5-7.5% in 2006
GDP growth: –1% to –3% GDP fall	GDP growth: 1.5%	GDP growth: 4-5%	GDP growth: 3.5-4.5%	GDP growth: 3.5-4.5%	GDP growth: 3.5-4.5%
Exchange rate: in 1999 the exchange rate was not a formal monetary policy target	Exchange rate: in 2000 the exchange rate was not a formal monetary policy target	Exchange rate: in 2001 the exchange rate was not a formal monetary policy target	Exchange rate: *nominal* exchange rate targeting?	Exchange rate: "The Bank of Russia believes that the ruble's REER may safely rise by 4% to 6% in 2003."	Exchange rate: "[T]he REER of the ruble may rise by 3%-5%. The Bank of Russia *will* try to stop it from rising by more than 7%."

Source: Esanov, Merkl & Vinhas de Souza (2005).

Institutional and structural factors have been constraining the effectiveness of monetary sterilisation. Only a limited set of sterilisation instruments is available to the CBR: after the domestic default of 1998, open market operations with government securities and CBR bonds were not carried out until 2003, owing to the sheer lack of marketable government securities in the CBR portfolio. In addition, the relatively shallow domestic financial market, with a large share of state-owned banks (see Box 2.3) operating under permanent excess liquidity, restricts the effectiveness of a monetary policy based on interest rates (Vinhas de Souza, 2006).

Box 2.3 The Russian banking system

Russia currently has 1,135 institutions authorised to perform banking operations (1,091 of which are banks, and of those 60 are foreign-owned or participated), down from 2,457 at the end of 1994. Among these, 909 banks or approximately 84% of the total (accounting for nearly 99% of all household deposits) were accepted into the deposit insurance scheme introduced in 2003, which was used to eliminate some of the undercapitalised banks that had previously plagued the Russian banking system.

The banking sector in Russia continues to be dominated by the state: the share of state-owned banks in the total banking sector assets at the end of 2005 was about 38%. The two largest banks, Sberbank (of which the CBR, another Gosbank offspring, is the major shareholder and which was effectively used as a policy tool by the CBR in the 1994–95, 1998 and 2007 crises) and Vneshtorgbank (VTB),[†] increased their market share in 2005 (to about 29% and 6% of the assets, respectively). So too did the rest of the state banks (to 3.5%, of which over 2% is accounted for by the Bank of Moscow, controlled by the Moscow city government). In addition, there are banks controlled by state-controlled corporations, the largest being Gazprombank with 5% of the sector's assets, and banks in which the state holds a non-controlling minority stake. Thus, estimates show that over 50% of the banking sector's assets are controlled directly or indirectly by the Russian state. It is usually assumed that state-controlled banks may not be as sensitive to interest rate changes as private ones, thereby hindering a monetary policy based on interest rates.

The counterpart of this large share of state control of the banking system is the *relatively* low share of foreign participation, which stood at around 16% of total assets in mid-2007,[††] in spite of the formal absence of limits on foreign ownership in the banking sector.[†††]

Box 2.3, cont.

Notwithstanding the dominant role of the state, no reduction of state ownership in the banking sector is foreseen in the Strategy for Banking Sector Development 2004–08, which was drawn up jointly by the Russian government and the CBR.

---

† As an indication of the willingness of the Russian state to consider *minority* private ownership even in such state bulwarks as Gazprom (whose ring-fenced limits to foreign ownership were removed in December 2005) and Rosneft (whose successful IPO occurred in 2006, attracting $10.6 billion), the IPO of some of Sberbank's capital was closed in February 2007, attracting around $9 billion in investment. VTB's own IPO happened in May 2007 and attracted a similar amount of money.

†† This share is indeed low if one compares it with the new EU member states. In Bulgaria, 80% of the assets of the banking system are foreign-owned, while the share is 95% in the Czech Republic, 98% in Estonia, 63% in Hungary, 68% in Latvia, 87% in Lithuania, 70% in Poland, 55% in Romania, 83% in Slovakia and 26% in Slovenia. *But Russia's share is actually not that low by the standards of comparably large EU economies* (7% in Germany and 15% in France) *and other large emerging economies* (2% in China, 8% in India and 27% in Brazil).

††† This policy is contrary to the insurance sector, where there is a quota for foreign participation currently set at 25%, which is expected to be lifted to 50% after accession to the World Trade Organisation. In any case, the foreign share of this sector is below that of banking.

Since the collapse of the sliding peg exchange-rate regime in 1998, the CBR has followed a managed exchange-rate regime, with parallel and incompatible inflation and exchange rate targets (with the exchange rate target usually considered to take precedence over the inflation target when inconsistencies arise). The ruble is currently pegged to a US dollar–euro basket. (In February 2005, the CBR started targeting a currency basket of initially 90% US dollars and 10% euros, with the CBR progressively increasing the euro share to reflect the EU's share in Russia's foreign trade; by February 2007, the euro share had reached 45%.)

So far, the CBR has been forced to follow a relatively accommodative monetary policy. The current external environment in Russia is a particularly challenging one for a central bank with such potentially inconsistent targets and limited tools at its disposal. The persistent and large current account surplus causes upward pressure on the exchange rate, which the CBR tries to prevent, to avoid missing its exchange rate appreciation target and thereby undermining the competitiveness of the non-natural resources sector. This, however, implies that the CBR has to buy up the large excess of dollars by selling rubles, with the consequence of permanent, excessive ruble liquidity on the domestic market, and hence potential inflationary pressures. Hard currency reserves at the CBR reached over $500 billion by late March 2008[70] (from around $182 billion in 2005) or the equivalent value of almost 18 months of imports. This figure makes Russia the third largest holder of hard currency reserves on the planet (after China and Japan).

Part of this expansion has been financed by the accumulation of *foreign private debt*. The *official* external debt-to-GDP ratio decreased further in 2006, from around 12% in 2005 to 4.7% (it had escalated to around 80% of GDP after the 1998 crisis), after a new round of debt pre-payment to the Paris Club in 2006, worth $22 billion (using StabFund assets), which followed the 2005 debt redemptions with the IMF and the Paris Club. Yet external debt has recently increased, owing to the strong accumulation of private and *quasi-private* (i.e. companies with state participation such as Gazprom, Rosneft, Sberbank and VTB) foreign debt: in 2006, it rose by over 20%, reaching $310 billion or almost 30% of GDP. By the end 2007, Russia's total external debt had reached almost $460 billion (a mere 10% of which is government debt).

This financial development was bolstered by the 2003 adoption of a law on the insurance of deposits (not implemented until 2005). This law is expected to promote more transparency in bank ownership, and improve banks' liquidity, solvency and capital adequacy as well as discipline in banking operations. Financial development is further supported by the CBR's shift of its supervisory procedures from compliance-based to risk-based supervision (shored up by a large and very successful TACIS[71] and

---

[70] In early 2007, Russia's currency reserves were roughly allocated as follows: 50% in US dollars, 40% in euros, 9% in British pounds sterling and 1% in Japanese yen.

[71] TACIS stands for Technical Aid to the Commonwealth of Independent States. It was the original EU assistance facility to support reform and development in the CIS countries (plus Mongolia), launched in 1991. Through it, the EU became one of the largest donors in the region (beyond TACIS, the EU has several support and technical assistance programmes in the region, from cross-border cooperation funds and European Investment Bank (EIB) external lending mandates to macro-financial assistance programmes, which are external adjustment packages managed by ECFIN that are similar to those of the IMF). With the end of transition and the 2004–07 EU enlargements, TACIS was replaced in 2007 by the more

European Central Bank technical assistance programme) and by the progressive introduction of international financial reporting standards (IFRS) and Basel-compatible capital adequacy ratios.

Another feature of the ongoing financial deepening in Russia is the expansion of its *equity market*. The equity market in Russia grew in value from $325 billion in early 2005 to over $1 trillion by the end of 2006, or from 53% to over 100% of GDP (far above the EU's average), while in 2002, the total capitalisation of the equity market in Russia had stood at a mere 25% of GDP.

A very substantial part of this boost is the result of the increase in the market value of energy-sector companies and the stock market flotation of state-owned ones. For instance, Gazprom increased its market valuation between mid-2005 and the first quarter of 2006 from $70 billion to $300 billion. During 2006–07, Russia was one of the best-performing stock markets in the world (see Figure 2.3).[72]

Since the full liberalisation of the capital account (which took place ahead of schedule on 1 July 2006),[73] the medium-term objective of the CBR has been the introduction of a floating exchange-rate-*cum*-inflation-targeting regime, which will free the monetary authority from considerations about the exchange rate. The recent reduction in the current account surplus, if continued, *may* imply a reduction of the structural excess liquidity, hence making monetary policy tools (including the CBR's refinancing of interest rates) more effective and reducing the dangers related to REER appreciation, such as a loss in competitiveness.

---

flexible and larger European Neighbourhood and Partnership Instrument (ENPI), the financial tool of the new European Neighbourhood Policy (ENP).

[72] There are 11 Russian stock exchanges in total: the Russian Trading System (RTS) and the Moscow Interbank Currency Exchange (MICEX), both in Moscow, plus 9 regional ones. A large share of stock trading is done away from the floors of the stock exchanges, however, through over-the-counter operations (see Vinhas de Souza, 2004b).

[73] Among other indications of the fuller financial integration of Russia into global financial markets, since early 2007 it has been possible to trade on US dollar/ruble futures, and Euroclear, an organisation that clears foreign exchange transactions, has begun accepting the ruble as a settlement currency on international transactions.

Figure 2.3 Russian Trading System stock index

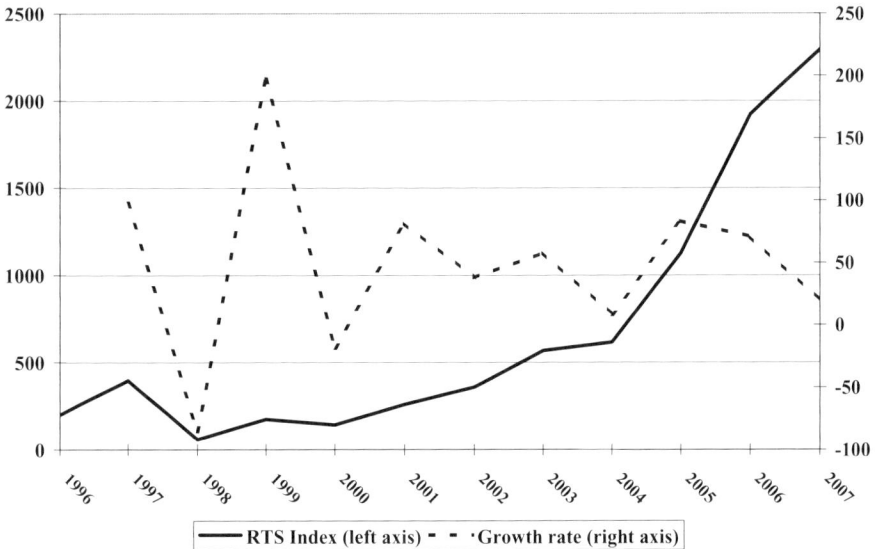

Source: RTS.

The 2007 CBR inflation target of 8% was missed, as inflation is estimated to have reached almost 12%, partially reflecting a worldwide commodities-driven price increase that has similarly affected several emerging markets, but the CBR has kept its 2008 target of 8.5%.

In order to contain the instability unleashed in financial markets by the collapse of the sub-prime mortgage market in the US, the CBR took various measures during August 2007, mirroring the actions of other central banks worldwide, including the European Central Bank and the Federal Reserve. These included the injection of a record RUB 1 trillion (over $40 billion) through repo operations during the second half of August 2007 in the banking system. Russia's large trade and current account surpluses make any significant liquidity provision operations by the CBR very rare. The CBR refinancing rate also went below the overnight money market rates in August (at 6% and 10%, respectively), reversing the usual spread between them. The CBR additionally sold around $5.5 billion in the domestic markets to deal with a lack of liquidity in US dollars. Those resources were taken from its hard currency reserves, as foreign investors repatriated some short-term capital from Russia in August (the outflow is estimated at around $5.6 billion). This caused a temporary break in the long-term appreciation trend of the ruble. The return of capital inflows by October and the usual injection of liquidity through budgetary execution in December 2007 provided further liquidity to the banking system.

As of March 2008, there are no significant indications that this market instability will have long-term effects in Russia (the 'decoupling' as discussed in relation to the experience of other emerging markets). Most of the likely channels of transmission of the instability are of a *microeconomic* character, and not macroeconomic as in 1998, given the much-improved macroeconomic situation and prospects of Russia. Concerning the micro channels, the Russian companies with the largest external liabilities are 'naturally hedged' (i.e. they have income flows in hard currency, as most are exporters of natural resources), which limits their vulnerability.

The major exceptions to this are banks, which have been responsible for a large share (perhaps as high as 50%) of the significant accumulation of private and quasi-private external liabilities in the last few years. Even so, there are mitigating factors in their case:

1) the fact that the largest Russian banks are majority state-owned. Indeed, the banks that seemed to face liquidity problems in August–September 2007 were a few private ones, a result similar to the estimations in Vinhas de Souza (2006); and

2) the limited exposure of Russian financial institutions to mortgage-backed securities, the main financial instruments behind the crisis.

The CBR has followed a measured route towards a more flexible exchange rate and a monetary policy centred on the slow reduction of inflation, but it also has responsibilities towards the stability of the financial system. The initial indications are that it reacted effectively to the financial instability episode initiated in August 2007, but perhaps at the cost of re-stoking inflation. In any case, it is likely that the most pressing challenge for monetary policy (and for economic policy in Russia) in the medium term is a switch in the external position, with the reduction and eventual disappearance of the current account surplus (forecast by ECFIN to occur as early as 2009). These changes would leave the country vulnerable to the run down of hard currency reserves and StabFund assets and to developments in capital inflows, the latter of which are considered in the next section.

2.3 Foreign direct investment[74]

As indicated above, until recently Russia has managed to grow with comparatively little investment. Russia has traditionally underperformed against other Eastern European and CIS countries in terms of FDI attraction. This situation has changed, with the share of net FDI in GDP reaching a value similar to that of other large emerging economies (such as China). The main issue, however, is the extent to which this surge in FDI will be short-lived or whether it will be sustained over time. This section describes the recent trends in terms of Russia's FDI inflows and outflows, the most important investors and the main sectors of destination.

2.3.1 Recent FDI performance

Prior to 2006, per capita FDI into Russia had been very disappointing, with Russia having significantly underperformed the CIS average since the early 1990s (Figure 2.4, top panel). In 2006, this situation changed abruptly, as net FDI per capita jumped above the 2005 level by almost 40 times.

This increase reflected a major jump in growth in total FDI inflows (see Figure 2.4, bottom panel). FDI into Russia had risen by almost 8.3 times since 2002, reaching around $29 billion in 2006,[75] or around 3.2% of GDP (more than three times its 2002 GDP share). Correspondingly, the share of

---

[74] This section is based on Vinhas de Souza (2008).

[75] The FDI series presented by the CBR and Rosstat are not always consistent (for instance, in 2006, the CBR indicated a total FDI figure of $28.7 billion, while Rosstat put it at $31.1 billion), owing to methodological differences. CBR data are on a balance-of-payments basis, differentiating between residents and non-residents and adjusting for exchange rate movements. Rosstat data are survey-based and without adjustment for the ruble appreciation. The data above come from the CBR. On the other hand, as Rosstat statistics are the only ones that can provide a breakdown by country of origin and sector of investment, they are used in Tables 2.3 and 2.4. Rosstat's longer foreign investment series classifies as "foreign investment" an aggregate of FDI, portfolio investment and "other investments" (this last item, in Rosstat's definition, includes "trade and other credits", which have grown from 40% of all foreign investment in 2000 to almost 76% in 2007). Rosstat *FDI* and *portfolio investment* statistics are significantly lower than the statistics given by the CBR. Also, Rosstat FDI data with a sector/country breakdown were only available to this author for 2006-07.

Russia in total FDI in the CIS, which had fallen during most of the 1990s, had escalated from under than 40% in 2002 to almost 70% in 2006 (which is still less than Russia's current share of the CIS aggregate GDP, at around 76%).

Figure 2.4 FDI in Russia and the CIS ($)

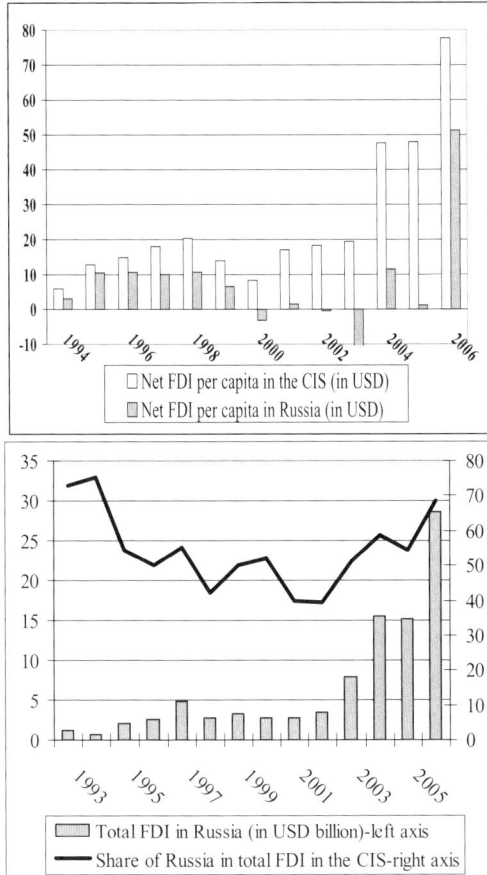

☐ Net FDI per capita in the CIS (in USD)
▨ Net FDI per capita in Russia (in USD)

▦ Total FDI in Russia (in USD billion)-left axis
━ Share of Russia in total FDI in the CIS-right axis

Sources: WDI, United Nations Economic Commission for Europe, CBR and author's own calculations.

The real change observed in 2006 was the sudden reversal of net FDI totals: net FDI and portfolio investment into Russia jumped from $-0.7 billion in 2005 to $+20.5 billion in 2006 (see Figure 2.5) or around 2.2% of GDP (at the same time, the item 'net errors and omissions' swings from $-8.8 billion to $1.1 billion). This is a very significant reversal of the traditional capital flight observed out of Russia, but at this stage, one cannot really speak of a sustained trend.[76]

Figure 2.5 Net FDI/portfolio and net total inflows ($ billion)

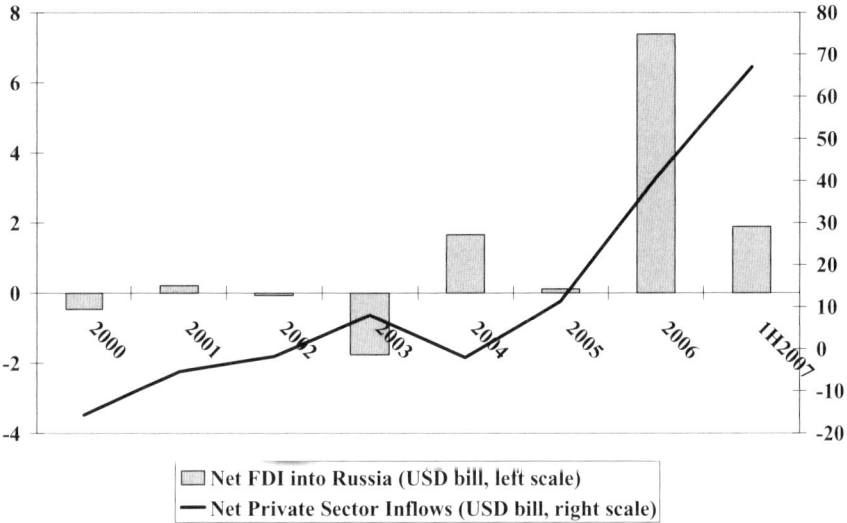

Net FDI into Russia (USD bill, left scale)
Net Private Sector Inflows (USD bill, right scale)

Sources: CBR and author's own calculations.

This trend seems to have continued in 2007, albeit not necessarily at the same scale (Figure 2.5).[77] Estimates by the CBR indicate that total FDI reached around $53 billion during 2007, while net FDI was around $7 billion. The balance of payments' surplus of the capital and financial account reached over $60 billion during the year. This increase in total inflows is partially explained by the launch of a number of large IPOs in the first half of 2007 (notably the IPOs of the two largest state-owned banks, Sberbank and VTB, which attracted around $9 billion each) and by the auction of the remaining assets of Yukos. The volume of capital inflows was forecast to abate during the remainder of 2007 even before the market

[76] According to the UN Conference on Trade and Development (UNCTAD, 2006), Russia had the third largest stock of outward FDI among emerging economies. Of course, outward FDI is not just 'capital flight'; it also reflects the (positive) increased internationalisation of an economy.

[77] UNCTAD (2007b) asserts that Russia is now the fourth most attractive *prospective* destination for FDI in the world.

turbulence of August 2007 (which seemingly had a very limited impact on capital inflows into Russia), because of more limited IPO-related activities, but the totals accumulated during the first nine months of 2007 were nonetheless very significant.

Total private sector inflows and outflows (i.e. including credit and loans) into Russia have systematically grown since 2000, with inflows surpassing outflows by 2003 (the positive balance by 2006 was almost $41 billion, for total inflows of over $105 billion). This increase is one of the factors behind the ongoing expansion in domestic investment, which is to some extent driven by state-controlled companies, and has as a counterpart the increase in foreign exposure of private and quasi-private companies. Throughout this period, Russian outward FDI and portfolio investment rose continually, from $3 billion in 2001 to almost $20 billion in 2006, as major Russian companies internationalised their operations (see Box 2.4).

Box 2.4 Russian transnational corporations

Russia is more and more a *source* of FDI, as discussed above (see Table B2.4a – using UNCTAD data, Russia held third place in terms of outward FDI stock in 2005, with $123 billion). This development is not necessarily negative, as a capital outflow is not always a sign of capital flight. Rather, it may show the growing integration of Russia into the world economy, as its companies expand abroad.

Table B2.4a Russian outgoing capital flows ($ billion)

	2000	2001	2002	2003	2004	2005	2006	2001–06
Total Russian FDI portfolio abroad	3.7	2.7	3.5	9.7	13.9	14.3	19.8	67.7
Sector outflows	19.1	11.8	19.8	25.4	40.9	60.2	64.8	241.9

Source: CBR.

Russia's largest companies (mostly in the natural resource sectors, but also in the financial and higher technological areas) compare favourably with the larger firms from other emerging markets (see Table B2.4b) and have led this process. The increased integration of Russian firms into the global economy is further represented by the growing number of IPOs in international financial centres (Severstal and Sintronics) and international mergers (for instance, the 2006 merger between the Swiss company Glencore and SuAl).

Box 2.4, cont.

Table B2.4b Ranking of Russian transnational corporations among CIS and south-eastern European transnational corporations, by foreign assets (2004)

Name	Rank	Sector	Assets abroad ($ million)	Sales abroad ($ million)	Employment abroad
Gazprom	1	Petroleum & natural gas	–	24,536	–
Lukoil	2	Petroleum & natural gas	7,792	26,408	13,929
Norilsk	3	Mining & quarrying	1,413	5,968	1,772
Novoship Co.	4	Transport	1,296	350	55
Rusal	6	Metal & metal parts	743	4,412	5,490
OMZ	7	Motor vehicles	347	271	8,484
Severstal	9	Metal & metal parts	174	3,954	7,098
Mechel	10	Metal & metal parts	120	2,203	10,689

Source: UNCTAD.

It is difficult to obtain precise information about the country and sector distribution of outgoing Russian FDI, but 5% of the Russian FDI in 2003–05 was invested in other CIS countries. Table B2.4c provides a list of recent, large foreign investments undertaken by Russian firms.

Table B2.4c Examples of large outgoing FDI by Russian transnational corporations in 2006–07

Investor	Industry	Company	Share acquired (%)	Value of deal ($ million)
Evraz	Steel	Oregon Steel Mills (US)	100	2,300
VTB	AeroSpace	EADS (France/Germany)	5	1,170
NLMK	Steel	Steel Invest (Finland)	50	805
Vimpelcom	Mobile telecom	Armentel (Armenia)	90	436
Norilsk Nickel	Metals	Nickel business of OM Group (US)	100	408
Interros	Energy	US Plug Power (US)	35	241
Rusal	Construction	Strabag SE (Austria)	30	1,500
AirBridge	Airline	Malev (Hungary)	100	210
Rusal	Metals	Alscon (Nigeria)	77.50	n.d.

Note:: n.d. refers to not disclosed.

Sources: Oxford Analytica, Intelli News and compilations by the author.

2.3.2   Origins of FDI inflows

Who is behind this sudden increase in investment? Although it is difficult to ascertain the sources precisely, it seems likely that a very significant share of both the investment inflows into Russia and the recent increase is *Russian capital* returning to the country through tax havens for tax 'optimisation' purposes. One can see that clearly in Table 2.3, which shows the most important sources of investment inflows into Russia by country.

Table 2.3 Sources of investment into Russia

	1995	2000	2002	2003	2004	2005	2006	3Q 2007
UK	6	6	12	16	17	16	13	24
Netherlands	3	11	6	6	13	17	12	20
Cyprus	1	13	12	14	14	10	18	14
Luxembourg	0	2	6	8	21	26	11	9
France	4	7	6	13	6	3	6	5
Germany	10	13	20	15	4	6	9	4
Virgin Islands (UK)	1	1	7	5	2	2	4	2
Switzerland	15	7	7	4	4	4	4	9
US	28	15	6	4	5	3	3	2
Others	33	25	19	17	15	15	28	23

Sources: Rosstat and author's own calculations.

As much as 18% of all investment inflows in 2006 and 14% in the first half of 2007 originated in Cyprus, one of the smallest EU member states.[78] Nearly one-third of the total 2006 investment and over a quarter during the first nine months of 2007 (and almost 35% of the total FDI stock by that date) originated in EU member states or EU-linked territories with similar

---

[78] The share of Cyprus in the FDI stock in September 2007 was 31%. Cross-checking Rosstat data with data from the Central Bank of Cyprus (CBC) lends supports to the notion that this is Russian capital 'round-tripping'. More specifically, the CBC only classifies as 'Cypriot' investment capital from companies and individuals satisfying some residence criteria, and the CBC data are equivalent to a mere 7.2% of the inflow that Rosstat labelled as Cypriot in 2005 (the average for 2002–05 was under 3.5%).

conditions for the taxation of capital (Cyprus, Luxembourg[79] and the UK Virgin Islands). In any case, the result is a consistently very high share of investment going into Russia from EU countries and territories: by September 2007, over 80% of investment inflows (and a similar figure for the stock) was from the eight most important EU-based investors.[80]

2.3.3 Sectoral distribution of investment inflows

Which sectors of the Russian economy attract the most investment flows? As shown in Table 2.4, the service sectors have consistently been the largest receivers of foreign investment, with between 50% and nearly 60% of the total investment inflows during 2003–07. Among the industrial sectors, the natural resource sectors and manufacturing attract roughly comparable amounts of investment. The investment in the energy sector fell sharply in 2005 following the Yukos affair. It has since partially recovered (in 2006 and 2007). The weight of foreign investment in energy in total foreign investment is close to the weight of the energy sector in Russia's GDP. This is also the case for foreign investment into manufacturing, which broadly reflects the GDP share of the manufacturing sector.

The share of the energy sector is much larger in *FDI* alone (i.e. without portfolio and 'other investments'). Cumulated FDI in the energy sector in September 2007 represented one-third of all FDI, slightly under that of the services sector. Also, the share of the energy sector in the FDI inflows in the period January–September 2007 was nearly two-thirds of the total (64%). That being said, the limitations of the Rosstat FDI data should be stressed once again.

Available statistics do not fully allow the geographical origin of the investment inflows to be cross-referenced with their sectoral destination. Nevertheless, in almost all sectors of the Russian economy, investment stemming from the EU member states seems to account for the largest share of the FDI total.

---

[79] Luxembourg also functions as a hub for FDI flows into the euro area, with a significant share of the FDI flowing into it going through Luxembourg-based 'special purposes entities' used for financial intermediation.

[80] Actually, when the Eurostat data on total EU FDI into Russia are cross-checked with the Russian series of *total* received FDI, EU FDI is more than 100% of the total FDI into Russia in some years.

Table 2.4 Sectoral distributions of FDI inflows into Russia, 2005–07 (%)

	2003	2004	2005	2006	3Q2007
Agriculture, hunting and forestry	0.5	0.3	0.2	0.6	0.3
Mining and quarrying	19.3	24.5	11.2	16.6	17.3
including					
mining and quarrying of energy-producing products	17.3	21.6	9.6	14.1	16
mining and quarrying, except energy- producing products	2	2.9	1.6	2.5	1.3
Manufacturing	22	25.3	33.5	27.5	24.6
of which					
manufacture of food products	3.4	2.3	2.2	2.5	2.5
manufacture of chemicals and chemical products	1.2	1.9	2.7	2.8	1.2
manufacture of metals and fabricated metal products	10.3	12.6	6.4	6.8	12.6
manufacture of transport equipment	0.7	2.1	1.8	2.6	0.9
manufacture of coke and mineral oil	0.6	0.2	15.1	7.2	3.8
Services	58.2	49.9	55.1	55.3	57.8
construction	0.3	0.6	0.4	1.3	1.2
wholesale, retail, repair activities	36.1	32.9	38.2	23.7	42.3
transport and communication	3.8	5	7.2	9.6	6.5
of which					
communication	2.3	3.4	6.1	8.5	2.9
financial intermediation	2.6	2.5	3.4	8.5	2.4

Sources: Rosstat and author's own calculations.

To ensure that the recent increase in FDI inflows – for which the EU is largely responsible – becomes a sustainable long-term trend, Russia still has to improve the overall investment climate in the country along with the legal framework for FDI. This subject is the focus of the next section.

2.3.4 Reforms in FDI legislation

The reform of the energy sector in Russia is tightly bound with the wider question of the legal framework for FDI. This legal framework for FDI in Russia is still being developed in several different directions, and not necessarily towards practices that are more restrictive.

The reforms have included the introduction of laws for research zones (technoparks) and industrial special economic zones (SEZs, after the 22 June 2005 federal Law on Special Economic Zones in the Russian Federation)[81] and for public–private partnerships,[82] after the 21 June 2005 federal Law on Concessions). These are potentially useful instruments for regional development and for attracting foreign investment into certain areas (for instance, infrastructure) that the government does not intend to privatise, if used in an exceptional and means-tested manner, and made strictly compatible with any international legal obligations undertaken by Russia (including accession to the World Trade Organisation (WTO)). Nevertheless, arguably the main outstanding questions related to FDI are investment in strategic sectors and the Subsoil Law.

In July 2007, the Russian government submitted to the State Duma the draft law on the rules for foreign investment in enterprises having strategic importance for the national security of the Russian Federation. This legislation has been in preparation since the summer of 2005. It comprises the Law on Strategic Enterprises and amendments to the Subsoil Law (the latter was first submitted to the Duma in 2005; it is still pending a first reading there). The draft states that in sectors deemed "strategic" (currently 39, albeit many of these are just sub-sectors of an industry),[83] foreign acquisition of *more* than 50% of the capital would require

---

[81] Technoparks were set up in Zelenograd, Tomsk, St Petersburg and Dubna, while industrial SEZs were approved for the Elabyga and Lipetsk regions. Resident companies in these SEZs are exempted from taxes on property and land, and from VAT and customs duties on imported equipment. Companies in industrial SEZs pay lower taxes on profits and on R&D, while those in technoparks pay half of the single social tax. The local and federal budgets also finance the building of infrastructure in the zones. In addition, several SEZs for tourism and recreational purposes were approved. A SEZ existed before this legislation in the Kaliningrad region.

[82] Public–private partnerships (PPPs) are justified more in terms of economic efficiency than for increasing a government's fiscal envelope. The largest example in Russia so far is the Western High Speed Diameter highway in St Petersburg, a project co-financed by the EBRD and the EIB.

[83] These sectors concern the hydro meteorological and geophysical industry, activities related to the use of pathogens of infectious diseases, the nuclear and airspace industries, the coding/cryptographic and surveillance industry, the military industry and the production/sales of goods and services from natural monopolies.

government authorisation (to be provided by a federal committee and within a maximum time limit of three months). For subsoil, an authorisation for foreign *majority* ownership would be necessary for deposits larger than a specific size.

Many international observers and enterprise associations (including the Association of EU Businesses in Russia) support these reforms as an attempt to centralise and clarify the legal framework that has otherwise remained largely ad hoc and dispersed among different organisations and administrative levels in Russia. At the same time, these observers note that the intended legislation has shortcomings. The major one in the current draft is a very broad definition of activities having "strategic significance for Russia's national security". Another is a lack of clarity on the potential retroactive effects of the new legislation. The government draft passed the first of the three necessary readings before the State Duma in September 2007, but it was withdrawn before its second reading in early November, apparently for more amendments, further delaying its approval process. It is unlikely that the approval procedures will advance before the end of the current transition in political power by mid-2008.[84] In the meantime, from an investor perspective, the fact that the Russian legal framework is currently not stable may be an even stronger deterrent to investments than its relatively restrictive nature.

On the other hand, significant progress has been observed in the liberalisation and reform of even some energy-related areas, such as the electricity sector (see Box 2.5). In any case, the gas sector (the subject of the next section) undeniably remains mostly unreformed.[85]

---

[84] In fact, another draft of the law was submitted in March 2008 to the Duma, which increased the list of strategic sectors by including media and telecommunications, eliminated some procedural improvements and reinforced the role of the Federal Security Service (FSB) in the vetting decision. This draft also incorporated into this law the Subsoil Law, with significant lower limits for foreign participation in the extraction sectors (albeit excluding majority state-owned enterprises of these new lower limits, effectively enabling Gazprom and Rosneft to continue their strategy of attracting foreign minority partners). This draft law passed its second reading in the Duma on 21 March 2008.

[85] It should be noted that Gazprom has a minority of foreign capital, and that the German company E.ON Ruhrgas AG actually has a seat on its board (and 3% of its capital). What the Law on Gas Supply regulating Gazprom says is that the Russian state must own 50% plus one share of its capital.

Box 2.5 Reforms in RAO-UES

Contrary to the gas sector, the electricity sector has undergone significant (if still incomplete) reform and opening-up in Russia. It is centred on one company, RAO-UES (a name that includes both the Russian and English acronyms of the company Unified Energy System). RAO-UES is the largest Russian power company, generating 69.4% (or 635.8 billion kWh) of the electricity and 32.4% (468.8 million Gcal) of the heating in Russia. It also owns 96% of the high-voltage grids and 77% of the distribution network in the country. It is one of Russia's largest companies, with almost 600,000 employees.

The sector initially underwent significant reform with the 11 July 2001 Law on Restructuring the Electric Power Industry of the Russian Federation, but the ageing infrastructure and the investment needs caused by the expansion of the Russian economy, sharply revealed by countrywide power shortages during the unusually cold winter of 2006, led to a renewed impulse for reform.

The new structure proposed by the 2001 law progressively separated the company into different functional segments (the unbundling of generation and power transmission), aimed at privatising in a staggered fashion the potentially competitive areas (mainly power generation), while keeping the 'natural monopoly' ones (such as power distribution grids) in state hands. RAO-UES is now a holding that owns the state share in these newly created companies.

The trunk (i.e. main) grids were integrated into a Federal Grid Company (100% owned by RAO-UES), while the distribution grids were transferred into new interregional distribution grid companies. RAO-UES also owns 100% of the System Operator – Centralised Dispatching Administration, which will oversee the liberalised wholesale and retail electricity markets.

The energy generation assets were consolidated into two types of interregional companies: generation companies for the wholesale market (OGKs in Russian) and territorial generation companies (TGKs in Russian). OGKs include mainly electrical power generation plants, while TGKs include combined heat and power plants, which generate both electrical and thermal power.

The reorganisation of the assets was mostly complete by 2006: seven OGKs, four interregional distribution grid companies and fourteen TGKs were established. That year, four TGKs and four OGKs were admitted to the Russian Trading System. In November 2006, OGK-5, in which RAO-UES had previously held an 87.67% stake, floated 14% of its stock for domestic and foreign investors, raising $459 million on the Russian Trading System and the Moscow Interbank Currency Exchange.

Box 2.5, cont.

Several IPOs occurred in 2007 and more are planned. In the most recent one, E.ON Ruhrgas AG acquired a 47.4% stake in the wholesale generator OGK-4 in mid-September 2007, in the largest FDI in the electricity sector ever made in Russia, worth around $4 billion. In another noteworthy development, in late August 2007, the Italian firm Enel acquired full control of OGK-5, in a $1.5 billion investment.

Parallel to the changes in market structure, a significant reform of the pricing policies was also approved: the wholesale electricity market was transformed into one based on regulated price/quantity contracts concluded between buyers and generation companies, while a limited electricity spot market was created. In addition, contracts with regulated prices are to be fully replaced by unregulated ones in 2011. This gradual liberalisation of retail markets is planned take place in conjunction with the wholesale market liberalisation (during the transition period, household electricity tariffs for the population will remain regulated).

2.4 Reforms in the energy sector in Russia: Gazprom

The energy sector in Russia holds particular interest for the EU, given the strategic importance of Russia as an energy supplier, especially of gas (the EU draws around 40% of its total gas imports from Russia, albeit this share has been falling). Moreover, given the size of the gas reserves (over three generations, at current exploration levels, as opposed to less than one for oil), gas has the potential to be a medium-term driver for growth in Russia if the sector is adequately reformed. In addition, despite the recent development of the state-controlled company Rosneft, the structure of the oil sector remains essentially private and competitive (as discussed in Box 1.2 above).[86] This section therefore focuses on the gas sector.[87]

The Russian gas industry has never truly departed from the market structure inherited from the Soviet period. Prices are regulated, exports are monopolised and the domestic market is dominated by a state-controlled, vertically integrated monopoly, Gazprom, which frequently seems to behave more like an arm of the Russian state than a company (see Box 2.6).

---

[86] There are, however, many outstanding questions concerning the legal framework for foreign participation in the exploration of oil fields in Russia.

[87] This focus in no way means that other utility monopolies in Russia (for instance, rail transport) are not in need of continued reform, liberalisation and opening-up.

As outlined in Box 1.2 above, Gazprom holds nearly one-third of the world's natural gas reserves, produces around 84% of all Russia's natural gas, controls almost all gas exports, supplies gas for the generation of close to 50% of the country's electricity and operates its own natural gas pipeline grid. Gazprom is also Russia's largest individual earner of hard currency, and the company's tax payments account for almost 25% of total federal tax revenues.

Box 2.6 (Min)GazProm – A brief history

The joint stock company (OAO) Gazprom was established in February 1993, after a presidential decree of 5 November 1992 and the Resolution of the Council of Ministers of 17 February 1993. It is the successor of the former Soviet Union's Ministry of Gas Industry (appropriately called MinGazProm). It combines commercial and regulatory functions. Its major shareholder is the Russian government, but since 1996, its shares have been traded on the Moscow stock exchange, and in December 2005, the limit for private ownership of its capital was increased to just below 50%, as a step in the process of opening the possibility for foreign participation in the company.

Gazprom is the world's largest gas-producing company and the third largest in terms of market capitalisation (after Exxon-Mobil and GE). It is responsible for around 8% of Russian GDP. It is the 100% owner of 58 subsidiaries (as of 1 September 2002) and it participates in the capital of almost 100 Russian and foreign companies. Together with its subsidiaries, its employees total nearly 300,000.

Its major gas fields are in the Nadym-Pur-Taz region of the Yamal-Nenetsk Autonomous Area, in Western Siberia, but it still produces about 7% of its gas in European Russia. In the future, the Yamal peninsula is expected to become its basic gas-producing region.

Gazprom also operates the Russian United Gas Transmission System, which encompasses 150,000 gas main lines and branches, 253 compressor stations with a total installed capacity of 42.6 million kW and 22 underground gas storage facilities. Gas is distributed from its network to regional systems through 3,633 distribution stations.

Through Gazprom, Russia controls gas supply routes and exports from the Caspian and Central Asian regions to Europe, through a series of bilateral deals with Kazakhstan, Turkmenistan and Uzbekistan spanning durations of up to 25 years. Under the current agreements, Russian imports from the three countries would amount to 115.5 bcm.

Despite its size and significance, Gazprom is seriously limited by domestic over-regulation, and the company can be almost absurdly inefficient.[88]

Concerning the legal framework under which it operates, Gazprom must supply the natural gas used to heat and power Russia's domestic market at government-regulated prices (approximately $25 per thousand cubic metres), regardless of profitability (two-thirds of Gazprom's profits come from its exports). Domestic gas prices, in spite of recent increases, remain below cost-recovery levels, implying significant subsides to the economy. Therefore, Gazprom's virtual monopoly in the sector is sometimes seen as a trade-off for the below-cost supply to domestic Russian households and industry. Following the agreement with the EU on Russia's WTO accession, however, domestic gas prices are bound to rise significantly. A freer market has also been established in principle in Russia, where Gazprom as well as oil companies and independent gas producers could sell gas at higher prices.[89] Nevertheless, various attempts to split Gazprom and further liberalise the domestic gas market have failed so far.

Recently, Gazprom has been trying to extend its influence throughout the CIS countries, raising its traditionally subsidised gas prices in the region to levels closer to those charged to the EU. It has used these price increases as a tactic to acquire full ownership of the transportation network towards its EU markets, by letting national energy companies in the CIS countries accumulate payment arrears. The acquisition of Moldovagaz, the gas company of Moldova, is a classic example of this strategy (see also Box 2.7, for a description of the disputes with Western CIS and Caucasus countries).

---

[88] For instance, the sector (i.e. the company) systematically comes at the bottom of the tables describing productivity gains in Russia, with annual productivity *losses* of almost 10% annually for the period 1997–2003. These losses are shown together with (related) increases of unit labour costs *above* 50% per year for the period 1997–2004 (Gazprom has the highest unit labour costs of all the Russian industrial sectors).

[89] At the end of November 2006, a cabinet decision was taken to liberalise the domestic electricity price fully by 2011. Equally, domestic gas prices in Russia are to reach $100 for 1,000 cubic metres by 2011, in staggered increases.

Box 2.7 Gazprom and gas prices in the CIS

Armenia

The price of natural gas received by Armenia from Russia doubled to $110 per trillion cubic metres (tcm) from 1 April 2006. Armenia concluded an agreement with Gazprom to maintain this still relatively low price for natural gas in exchange for the transfer of ownership of parts of the country's energy infrastructure on a temporary basis. Under this deal, the delivery price and terms will remain unchanged until 1 January 2009. The assets transferred from Armenian to Russian control include a thermal power plant and, reportedly, part of the new gas pipeline to Iran (Gazprom, through a joint venture, was granted the concession to build a larger, second pipeline along this route as part of the agreement). Other thermal power plants were transferred to Russia's United Energy System (RAO-UES) in 2002–03, as part of the debt-for-assets deal that settled Armenia's $96 million debt to Russia. Gazprom is also expected to increase its share in the Armenian gas transport company ArmRosGazprom from the current 45% to 58% (a further 10% is already owned by Itera, a Russian energy trading company that is active throughout the former Soviet Union and has ties to Gazprom). Therefore, nearly all of Armenia's energy infrastructure is now controlled by Russian companies.

Belarus

In December 2006, Gazprom indicated that it would stop gas supplies via Belarus (the second most important transit country to EU markets, responsible for around 15% of Russian deliveries to the EU), unless agreement was reached on a substantial increase in the price paid (from the very low $46.7 per tcm) and a joint venture with BelTransGaz, the Belarusian state-owned gas transmission company. An agreement was reached just before the deadline of 31 December 2006, avoiding the suspension of gas supplies. The new agreement covers the period 2007–11. The gas price for 2007 is $100 per tcm. From 2008, this price will be linked to the prices charged to the EU, minus transportation costs. It will be 67% of this price in 2008, 80% in 2009, 90% in 2010 and 100% in 2011. Transit fees for 2007 were set at $1.45, up from $0.75 per tcm/100 km in 2006. Gazprom also agreed on a price of $2.5 billion for a 50% stake in a joint venture with BelTransGaz, to be paid in instalments over the next four years. [†]

Georgia

Russia was Georgia's main gas supplier until 2006. In December 2006, the prices for Russian gas imports more than doubled from $110 to $235 per tcm. Yet the new South Caucasus (Baku–Tbilisi–Erzerum) gas pipeline will enable Georgia to diversify its gas supply: Georgia is expected to receive 250 million cubic metres (mcm) from Azerbaijan through this pipeline in 2007. There is an agreement to increase this amount by 100 mcm per year thereafter. This increase is likely to lower the average price for Georgian gas imports.

Box 2.7, cont.

Although there is little official information on Georgia's arrangements with its alternative suppliers – Azerbaijan and Turkey for 2007 – it is known that since the beginning of 2007 Georgia has been receiving Azerbaijani gas through an older pipeline, reportedly for about $120. Turkey's gas may also play a role, if an agreement to sell some of one of its pipeline quotas is reached.

Moldova

The gas sector in Moldova is controlled by Moldovagaz, 51% of which was transferred to Gazprom in return for the cancellation of arrears due from the company (i.e. ultimately, the Moldovan government) to Gazprom. Gazprom requested a twofold price increase as of 1 January 2006, and after extensive negotiations with the Moldovan government, the import price for gas was settled at $110 per tcm for the first half of 2006. During the second half of that year, prices were again raised to $160 per tcm (average prices for 2006 were around $135). A transit fee of $2.5 per tcm was charged for transit services provided to Gazprom by Moldovagaz. In December 2006, Gazprom and Moldovagaz signed a five-year agreement on gas deliveries to Moldova, valid until 2011. Under this agreement, Gazprom raised the price to $170 per tcm. For 2007, the contracted volume has remained roughly constant at the 2006 level of 2.5 bcm (total imports in 2006 were 2.3 bcm, of which around 0.9 bcm were used by the breakaway region of Transnistria, with the result that only around 1.4 bcm were used by Moldova proper). The transit tariff for Russian gas exports via Moldova remains unchanged. Moldova transits on average 20 to 22 bcm of Russian gas annually to Balkan countries (mainly to the EU member state of Romania). Mirroring the situation in Belarus, this five-year agreement with Gazprom also stipulates a gradual increase in the price to a European 'average price' minus transportation costs. Under this agreement, Gazprom will charge Moldova 75% of that price in 2008, 85% in 2009, 90% in 2010, and 100% in 2011. As part of the agreement, Moldova transferred the ownership of its domestic gas distribution networks to Gazprom, as a way to reduce further the remaining accumulated arrears.

Ukraine

In December 2005/January 2006, a very heated dispute arose between Russia and Ukraine concerning a request by Gazprom to increase the gas price charged to Ukraine, from $50 per tcm to $230 in January 2006. Ukraine is the major transit country for Russian gas to its EU markets and is responsible for about 80% of total deliveries. (Ukraine transited about 115 bcm of gas until 2005 and received about 25-bcm worth of gas as a barter payment for that transit. The transit fee paid to Ukraine was $1.09 per tcm/100 km; by comparison, the EU transit fee was $2.6 per tcm/100 km in 2005.) Ukraine rejected Gazprom's offer, leading to the suspension of Russian gas deliveries to Ukraine on 1 January 2006.

Box 2.7, cont.

This suspension briefly affected some EU markets, as Ukraine sought to compensate for the reduction in Russian deliveries by siphoning off gas destined for the EU. An agreement was reached on 4 January 2006. Valid for five years, the agreement set prices at an average of $95 (for a combined aggregate of Russian and Turkmen gas) for 2006. Ukrainian transit fees were also increased by 47%, to $1.6 per tcm/100 km. All gas is now traded on a cash basis and all gas imports into Ukraine are now undertaken through a monopoly, RosUkrEnergo (a non-transparent company with headquarters in Switzerland). In late 2006, prices were raised again, to $130 per tcm. So far, Ukraine has resisted Gazprom's proposals for the transfer of ownership of its pipeline network.

In summary, despite of such significant energy price increases for countries largely dependent on Russian gas, the predicted negative growth effects have so far not materialised, largely owing to the accumulation of private and quasi-private external debt, plus other nationally specific factors (Lysenko & Vinhas de Souza, 2007).

---

† Not only did Belarus receive natural gas from Russia at well below the Western European rates, it also benefited from very specific arrangements in the oil trade (Lysenko & Vinhas de Souza, 2007). Belarus imported crude oil from Russia free of export duties, and exported refined oil products primarily to Western Europe at a large mark-up. According to the terms of a 1995 treaty, Belarus and Russia were supposed to unify export duties on oil and refined oil products and to share Belarusian export-duty revenues: 15% to Belarus and 85% to Russia. But Belarus charged lower export duties on exports of oil and refined oil products, violating the agreement. Moreover, Belarus did not transfer the corresponding revenue to the Russian budget, in spite of several complaints by the Russian government over the years: in 2005–06, the foregone revenue for Russia was estimated at over $1 billion per year. This situation generated substantial profits for some Russian companies that had transferred their refining operations to Belarus, and boosted Belarusian exports and fiscal revenues. In December 2006, shortly before the rise in gas prices, this offshore tax avoidance scheme with oil duties was ended by Russia. Tensions between the countries escalated in January 2007, and the standoff was only resolved on 12 January 2007. Later, in December 2007 Russia provided Belarus with a loan of $1.5 billion, to cushion the adjustment costs.

Source: Based on Lysenko & Vinhas de Souza (2007).

Beyond that, Gazprom has started a flurry of moves aimed at increasing its market presence in the EU, through acquisitions, bilateral deals, infrastructure construction and asset swaps with companies in several EU countries (Belgium, Bulgaria, the Czech Republic, France, Germany, Greece, Hungary, Italy, Lithuania, the Netherlands, Poland,

Portugal and the UK) (see Table 2.5). The company is also engaged in several deals, some of them rather *muscular* (see Box 2.8), towards the expansion of its production *and* transport capabilities within and outside Russia.[90] These deals are mainly focused on the Asian markets – especially China – as the overwhelming share of Gazprom's transport infrastructure is geared towards the EU market, which currently puts the EU in a near-monopsony position with respect to Gazprom.

Table 2.5 Gazprom's foreign subsidiaries and affiliates

Country	Company name	Types of operations	Gazprom's share (%)
Armenia	Armrosgazprom	Gas distribution	45
Austria	Gas und Warenhandelsgesellschaft	Sale of gas	50
Belarus	BelTransGaz	Gas distribution	50
Bulgaria	Overgaz	Gas distribution	23
	Overgaz Incorporated	Investing	50
	Topenergo	Gas distribution	100
Cyprus	Leadville Investments Ltd	Investing	100
Czech Rep.	Gas Invest	Investing	n.d.
Estonia	Eesti Gaas	Gas distribution	37
Finland	Gasum	Gas distribution	25
	North Transgas OY	Gas transportation	50
France	Fragaz	Gas trading	50
Germany	Wingas	Gas distribution	35
	WIEH	Gas distribution	50
	ZMB	Gas distribution	100
	GWH	Gas distribution	100
	ZGG	Gas distribution	100

---

[90] As an example of the expansion strategy within Russia, in October 2006 the Russian government awarded Gazprom a monopoly on the exploration of the giant Shtokman gas field in the Barents Sea, without the participation of the foreign partners (Statoil, Hydro, Conoco, Chevron and Total) that had been planning to bid for allocations in the field. Gazprom later announced that it could invite selected foreign firms as its subcontractors there (indeed, in July 2007 Gazprom allocated 24% of the Shtokman field to Total, and a similar share later in the year to Norsk Hydro). Another example is the selling of the TNK-BP share of the Kovytka oil and gas field to Gazprom in June 2007, a sale caused by TNK-BP's fears of losing the exploration licence for the field (admittedly for not complying with the terms of the licence).

Table 2.5, cont.

Greece	Prometheus Gas	Foreign trade	50
Hungary	Panrusgaz	Sale of gas	40
	Borsodchem	Petrochemical production	25
	DKG-EAST Co. Inc.	Gas trading	38
	TVK	n.d.	14
	General Banking and Trust	Investing	26
Italy	Promgaz	Gas distribution	50
	VOLT A S.p.a	Gas trading	49
Kazakhstan	KazRosGaz	Gas distribution	50
Latvia	Latvijas Gaze	Gas distribution	34
Lithuania	Lietuvos Dujos	Gas distribution	34
	Stella Vitae	Gas distribution	50
	Kaunasskaya power station	Electricity	99
Moldova	Moldovagaz	Gas distribution	50
Netherlands	Gazprom Finance B.V.	Investing	100
	Blue Stream Pipeline Co.	Construction, gas transport	50
	West–East Pipeline Project Investment	Construction, investing	100
Poland	EuRoPolGAZ	Gas distribution	48
	Gas Trading	Sale of gas	16
Romania	Wirom	Gas distribution	25
	WIEE	Gas distribution	50
Serbia	Progresgaz Trading Ltd	Gas distribution	25
	NIS	Gas distribution	51
Slovakia	Slovrusgas	Gas trading	50
	Slovensky Plynaremky Priemysel	Gas distribution	16
Slovenia	Tagdem	–	n.d.
Turkey	Turusgaz	Sale of gas	45
UK	Gazprom Marketing and Trading Ltd	Gas distribution	100
	Gazprom UK Ltd	Investing, banking	100
	Interconnector (UK) Ltd	Gas trading	10
	HydroWingas	Gas distribution	50

Note: n.d. refers to not disclosed.

Source: UNCTAD.

Box 2.8 Gazprom and Sakhalin II

The Russian Ministry of Natural Resources made a decision on 18 September 2006 to revoke the overall environmental permit for the Sakhalin II project, effectively threatening to shut down an investment worth tens of billions of US dollars. Sakhalin II is a very large venture undertaking gas exploration, transport, liquefied natural gas (the only such facility for the latter in Russia) and shipping situated in the Russian Pacific coast, designed to cater mainly for the Asian market. Sakhalin II is also covered by one of only three energy-sector Production Sharing Agreements that were signed during the 1990s.† The apparent reasons for the action were i) a cost overrun of $10 billion by the Shell-led project, which would have effectively denied the Russian government several billions of dollars in revenues, under the PSA terms; and ii) an overall perception of the PSAs as too advantageous for foreign investors.

The situation was resolved on 21 December 2006: Gazprom bought 50% plus one share of the project from the consortium partners, Royal Dutch Shell, Mitsui and Mitsubishi Corporation, for a reported $7.5 billion. The environmental suit was quietly dropped after that.

---

† PSAs are contracts that replace the existing tax and licence regimes with ad hoc arrangements that exist for the life of the project. PSAs were created in Russia in December 1993 by presidential decree, but the PSA Law was not enacted until 1995. Just three PSAs were ever signed:

- Sakhalin I, an oil and gas development on the northeast shelf of Sakhalin island, begun in late 2001. The consortium members are ExxonMobil (with 30%), the Japanese consortium SODECO (30%), Rosneft (20%) and the Indian state-owned oil company ONGC Videsh Ltd., with the remaining (20%);
- Sakhalin II (the first PSA signed, in 1996); and
- the sub-arctic oil field of Kharyaga, where Total holds a 50% stake and the Norwegian oil and gas company Norsk Hydro holds another 40%, while the state-owned Nenets Oil Company holds the remaining 10%. The Russian government has had the legal option of increasing its capital by 20% (10% from Total and 10% from Norsk Hydro) since 2007.

Beyond the financing needs for the deals outlined in the previous paragraph, the investment and depreciation needed for the continued development of the Russian gas sector are immense. The government's Energy Strategy of the Russian Federation for the period up to 2020 forecasts the need for investments in the order of $660–880 billion until 2020 (or $30–40 billion per year). To put these numbers in perspective, the combined capital expenditures of the largest companies in the sector

(Lukoil, Rosneft, TNK-BP, Surgutneftegaz, Gazprom Neft, Tatneft, Gazprom and NOVATEK) totalled $20.5 billion in 2005, and an estimated $21.5 billion in 2006.[91]

These very significant financing needs and the clear interest of Gazprom in entering the EU market may provide leverage for pressing for domestic liberalisation, if the EU manages to act fast and in a consistent fashion. In any case, domestic liberalisation should be pursued because it is welfare-improving for Russia itself.

The reform of the FDI framework is linked to another subject concerning Russia: the competitiveness of its economy. This topic is dealt with in the next section.

2.5 Competitiveness

Some studies indicate that resource-rich countries *may* grow at a slower pace than non-resource rich ones, in what is termed in the literature as the 'natural resource curse'.[92] Although such growth underperformance does not seem to be the case for Russia,[93] this issue is still worthy of policy-makers' attention.

Three main (non-exclusive) explanations are offered for the natural resource curse (Oomes & Kalcheva, 2007). The first is that natural resource wealth gives rise to rent-seeking behaviour, the second is that natural

---

[91] The combined capital expenditures of this group of companies increased quite significantly between 2004 and 2005, by almost 48% in nominal US dollar terms and by a further 4.6% in 2006. The state-owned companies (Gazprom and Rosneft) were responsible for almost 80% of this increase.

[92] Some studies do find that a high level of resource abundance leads to lower growth rates (see Sachs & Warner, 1995 – the literature classic – and Manzano & Rigobon, 2001). On the other hand, some papers question this finding and argue that, after correcting for *institutions*, no negative effects of primarily resources-led growth exist (see Gylfason et al., 1997; Gylfason, 2000; Matsen & Torvik, 2005; Arezki & van der Ploeg, 2007).

[93] As indicated previously, since 1999, Russia's growth performance has been quite close to the CIS and 'all transition' averages, and has comfortably surpassed the performance of the new EU member states, not to mention the EU average (see Figure 1.4 in section 1.4.1). Russia also performs far above a sample of resource-rich countries, as shown in Figure 1.14 in section 1.5.3.

resource dependence implies terms-of-trade volatility, while the third (and most common) is the Dutch disease.

According to the first explanation, resource wealth may generate a conflict over the existing resources, which leads to poor institutional quality and lower growth (in other words, the substantial rents that can be derived from the natural resources create incentives for governments and private agents to engage in unproductive rent-seeking behaviour, crowding out other activities). The second explanation is based on the empirical observation that natural resource prices tend to be volatile, and volatility is negatively correlated with growth and investment. Finally, the Dutch disease hypothesis is the notion that an exogenous increase in resource prices or output[94] results in a real exchange rate appreciation and ultimately a decline in the domestic manufacturing sector, while the services sector will expand (as manufactured goods are mostly tradable, while services are not, the price of manufactured goods are set on the world markets).[95]

The Dutch disease hypothesis also generates three testable implications (Oomes & Kalcheva, 2007): i) there is a fall in manufacturing output and employment, ii) real wages increase and iii) the real exchange rate appreciates (as the prices for services rise). How well these three features apply to Russia is considered below.

1)   *The share of manufacturing output and employment.* When considering these aspects for Russia, two provisos must be taken into consideration. First, centrally planned economies tend to have a higher share of industry in GDP than countries with comparable GDP per capita levels; therefore, the transition process is also a process of *relative* de-industrialisation. Second, as countries grow richer, the consumption basket (and hence production) switches to services, which grow in terms of GDP share. Thus, a catching-up process *also* implies a *relative* de-industrialisation.

With these provisos in mind, Table 2.6 shows that the share of manufacturing industry in GDP has remained roughly constant in

---

[94] In the original Dutch case that gave the disease its name, the increase stemmed from the discovery of large natural gas deposits off the coast of the Netherlands.

[95] The Dutch disease notion can be linked not only to any natural resource (including agricultural crops) but also to any increase in foreign exchange inflows, including international transfers (like EU funds and remittances), aid or loans.

Russia since 1999. Meanwhile, the industrial employment share in total employment has fallen marginally, by roughly 1%.

Table 2.6 Shares of industry and services in GDP and employment for Russia (%)

	1998	1999	2000	2001	2002	2003	2004	2005	2006	Avg.
Share of manufacturing industry in GDP	18.1	19	17.6	17.9	17.6	17.0	18.1	19.3	19.4	18.1
Share of services in GDP	64.4	61.5	55	56.7	59.5	59.7	59	60	58.2	59.3
Share of industrial employment	20.7	22.4	22.7	22.7	22.2	21.8	21.4	21.7	21.2	21.9
Labour productivity in industry	0.8	7.3	10.1	5	6.8	10.5	8.9	6.2	5.8	6.8
Real wage increase	73.8	10.9	22.4	27.1	19.5	12.8	12.3	14.4	14.6	6.7

Sources: EBRD, Rosstat and author's own calculations.

In other words, it is not clear that Russia has experienced either a loss in the share of its manufacturing industry in GDP or a reduction of industrial employment in total employment, at least since 1999, so Russia does not seem to reflect this Dutch disease symptom.

2)   *Wage increases.* Wages have indeed increased in Russia, but so far, this tendency has been outstripped by *productivity* increases. The average *real* wage increase during the 1998–2006 period was 6.7% per year, while the average yearly rise in labour productivity in industry for the same period was 6.8% (although the average productivity figures for this period are clearly bolstered by the 1998 devaluation). Figure 2.6, which shows the relative productivity of Russian industry against a composite benchmark of the EU and the US, reveals that Russian productivity has systematically grown compared with this benchmark, especially since its departure from the peg regime in 1998. Thus, the loss in competitiveness that one could expect from the Dutch disease is not observed in the data available (Oomes & Kalcheva, 2007).

Figure 2.6 Relative Russian productivity (100: 1995-01)

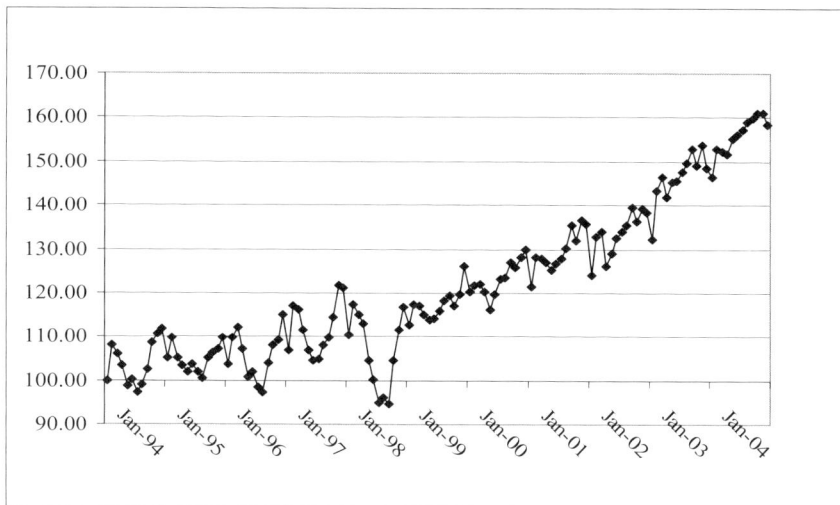

Sources: Author's estimations based on data kindly provided by Oomes & Kalcheva.

3)   *REER*. The real exchange rate has appreciated in Russia and is now above its pre-1998 level (see Figure 1.6 in section 1.4.3). One of the reasons for that is the higher inflation rate in Russia than in its trading partners and the substantial current account surpluses stemming from the commodities boom, which is consistent with the Dutch disease hypothesis. Nevertheless, another reason for the REER appreciation is that Russian productivity has grown faster than that of its partners (see again Figure 2.6). This is a common phenomenon in transition economies and those that are catching up, and is usually referred to as the Balassa-Samuelson effect (Oomes & Kalcheva, 2007). According to the Balassa-Samuelson hypothesis, the real exchange rate should appreciate in line with the relative productivity differentials as an equilibrium process. If productivity growth in the tradables sector exceeds productivity growth in the non-tradables sector, the prices of Russian non-tradables will rise over time, while the prices of Russian tradables will not (as the latter are determined by the world level). This implies a rise in the overall Russian price level, i.e. a real appreciation. Put differently, at least some of the

REER development in Russia is a necessary (and again, beneficial) equilibrium reaction to a catching-up process.[96]

The conclusion of this section is that a clear majority of analyses find it difficult to detect any clear symptoms of the Dutch disease in Russia,[97] although of course, given the potential negative effects of the Dutch disease, care should be taken to prevent it from developing. In any case, the issue of competitiveness is closely linked to the overall reform of the state apparatus as the latter affects incentives and defines the framework for investment, both domestic and foreign. This area of reform is briefly discussed in the next section.

2.6   Taming the leviathan: The reform of the Russian state

The reform of Russian state institutions is arguably the most important item on the country's reform agenda, especially in an environment of a seemingly activist state that seeks to create state-owned or backed 'national champions' (even if some policy statements may present this as a temporary stage for a future re-privatisation).

The reforms undertaken in the early 2000s by the Putin administration reorganised relations between the federal centre and the regions, and re-ordered the structure of the federal government itself. Since then, most of the recent efforts have been focused on reforming the courts, the civil service (through the Presidential Decree on Administrative Reform of July 2003) and the major regulatory institutions, and on their relations with the federal and regional governments (with both sets of reforms interrelated). Perhaps inevitably, progress in the implementation of these

---

[96] On the other hand, Habib & Kalamova (2007) find that there is a long-term relationship between the ruble real exchange rate and oil prices, although they caution that the shortness of the time series affects the interpretation of this result.

[97] An exception to this is the recent work by Ollus & Barisitz (2007). The authors, using a 2000–06 sample and working with EU–Russia imports (the EU supplies over 50% of Russia's total imports), claim to find signs of the Dutch disease, represented by a stronger growth of Russian imports from the EU than domestic production in some Russian industrial sectors. It should be noted that to assume this as a sign of Dutch disease implies a conclusion about the nature of imports, namely, whether they are *complements to* or *substitutes for* domestic production. As most Russian imports from the EU are of capital goods, they could be seen as complements to domestic production, and therefore necessary for the modernisation of Russian industry.

reforms has been uneven. While taxation and regulatory capabilities have indeed improved substantially (for the fiscal framework, see section 2.2 above), the same cannot be said for rule enforcement or other areas (OECD, 2006b and 2004) (see also Box 2.9).

Box 2.9 Some recent reforms in the Russian legal framework

- Amendments clarifying the law on *competition* were passed in September 2002.

- Concerning *intellectual property rights*, at present Russian legislation mostly matches international standards, after the corresponding section of the Civil Code was signed into law in December 2006.

- In September 2002, in collaboration with and supported by the World Bank, the European Commission (through the TACIS programme), the EBRD and the OECD, the Russian government changed the legislation on *corporate governance*.

- A new *bankruptcy* law was passed in the autumn of 2002, changing and clarifying the relations between creditors and debtors. It also toughened penalties for deliberate misinformation and false bankruptcy.

- Two laws against *money laundering* were passed in July 2001 and September 2002.

The main question concerning the significant legal changes above is their *enforcement*, which refers to the reform of the state apparatus discussed in this section.

Source: OECD (2006b and 2004).

Serious questions remain concerning the independence of the judicial and law enforcement systems and the state, as state bodies are sometimes 'captured' by private or sectoral interests. The Russian state bureaucracy is naturally multilayered (reflecting the size and complexity of the country) and often unresponsive to the needs of the population. At the least, it is viewed as being non-transparent, pervaded by corruption and beholden to interest groups (as plainly illustrated by the recent episode involving the Russian Ministry of Natural Resources, Gazprom, Shell and the Sakhalin II project previously described in Box 2.8).

An extensive reform of the Russian judicial system was undertaken in 2001 (Owen & Robinson, 2003). It included a new civil code and a new code for the arbitration courts, and new laws on the status of judges and on the constitutional court. A further step taken in the same year was the reduction and clarification of the role of the federal prosecutor's office. Even so, these efforts have not affected the overall perception of the unreliability of the Russian legal system, and some well-known cases seem to substantiate this impression (for instance, the recent jailing of a deputy minister of finance for corruption under rather unclear circumstances). [98] In any case, formal judicial independence has been strengthened by the new law on the status of judges, which raises judicial pay and establishes new mechanisms for punishing judicial malpractice. The federal government has also sought to improve the financing and training[99] of the judicial system, and has tried to reduce the dependence of judges on regional authorities (but tellingly, not to curtail the federal influence on them). In addition, a new tier of arbitration courts has been created (OECD, 2004).

In the end, there is a limited amount of external influence that can affect the reform of Russian state institutions. The feasible policy recommendation would be the continued support of the reformist institutions within the Russian government – the Ministry of Finance/MEDT, the CBR and the Federal Service for Financial Markets. Further recommendations are to engage consistently with other bodies of the wider Russian state structure at the federal and regional levels, and to use the international *fora* that enable the sharing of international best practice with the Russian government.

The full utilisation of these external anchors for reform is an important part of this strategy. Among these anchors are G8 participation, WTO accession,[100] OECD membership,[101] the future EU–Russia framework agreement that will replace the Partnership and Cooperation Agreement

---

[98] Even the newly elected Russian President, Dmitry Medvedev, called Russia a "country of legal nihilism" in a speech in January 2008.

[99] It was not until 1999 that the Russian Academy of Justice was founded, a body that provides training for judges in the Supreme and Arbitration Courts. It almost doubled its intake of trainees in 2005 to around 9,000 with the support of an EU TACIS programme (EBRD, 2007).

[100] Russia signed an agreement with the EU concerning its WTO Accession already in 2004.

[101] Russia was accepted for eventual OECD membership in May 2007. The European Commission is also a party of the OECD Convention, its founding charter, and therefore represented in this organisation.

(PCA),[102] an eventual EU–Russia deep free trade agreement after WTO accession, the EU–Russia Sectoral Dialogues initiated under the 2003 EU–Russia 'common spaces'[103] (including the EU–Russia Macroeconomic and Financial Issues Dialogue),[104] the EIB and the EBRD,[105] and of course, the

---

[102] The PCA has been the framework of the EU–Russia relationship for a decade. It was signed in 1994 and entered into force on 1 December 1997 for an initial period of 10 years; it was automatically extended for one year in 2007. The agreement regulates the political, economic and cultural relations between the EU and Russia and is therefore the legal basis for the EU's bilateral trade and investment with Russia. One of its main objectives is to promote trade and investment as well as the development of harmonious and sustainable economic relations between the parties. The PCA contains several special provisions regarding economic relations between the EU and Russia. Pending approval of a negotiating mandate by the European Council, it is expected in due course to be replaced by a framework agreement.

[103] At the St Petersburg summit in May 2003, the EU and Russia agreed to reinforce cooperation with a view to creating four EU–Russian common spaces in the context of the existing PCA. The common economic space aims at increasing opportunities for economic operators, a further step towards establishing a more open and integrated market between the EU and Russia. The three other spaces are the common space of freedom, security and justice; the common space on external security; and the common space on research, education and culture. They are complemented by the roadmap on the common economic space, adopted at the EU–Russia summit in Moscow on 10 May 2005. This document sets out a number of principles and priority activities. It also sets up various dialogues on specific issues, including economic and finance-related issues.

[104] This framework is the main channel between Russia and the European Commission for the discussion of macroeconomic and financial subjects, involving the Directorate-Generals for ECFIN and the Internal Market and Services, which is managed by this author at ECFIN. The 2007 meeting of this framework took place during October 2007 in Brussels. The next meeting is scheduled to take place in Russia during the fall of 2008.

[105] With respect to the EBRD, the anchor is effected through conditionalities in their projects. Under a Memorandum of Understanding concerning the EIB's so-called 'third external mandate', which covers the resources made available to it for investment in the Western CIS countries, the EIB and the EBRD shall act jointly in project preparation and acquisition in the areas traditionally covered by the EIB (such as infrastructure). One must note here that both the European Commission and the EIB have shares of EBRD's capital, and therefore seats on its board. In addition, EU member states, plus the European Commission and the EIB, have over 64% of EBRD's capital.

traditional Bretton Woods institutions.[106] The several EU–Russia Sectoral Dialogues, given their capacity and institutional mandate to interact comprehensively with multiple bodies of the Russian government, are perhaps uniquely qualified for such a deep sharing of best practice with Russian counterparts.

Nonetheless, the continued reform of the state must be pursued because it is in Russia's own interest. The lack of continued reform there is not only problematic in itself, it also calls into question the effectiveness of reform in all other areas, including the macroeconomic framework and financial sector in which Russia is recognised to have been relatively successful.

Finally, it should be recognised that any reforms inevitably have social costs, which are discussed in the next section.

2.7   Inequality and social reform

Transition had some initially wrenching social consequences in Russia. Open unemployment, almost unheard of during Communist times (albeit underemployment was substantial) jumped with the onset of the transformation period, from 0.08% in 1991 (effectively, full employment) to 5.3% in the following year, representing a 6,400% increase (and by 1998, it had more than doubled, to 13.3%). Poverty grew very significantly: using a World Bank usual poverty indicator (namely, the share of the population with a PPP-adjusted income of less than $2 a day), poverty in Russia rose from 2% in 1988 (admittedly a very low figure, which, like many USSR statistics, may have been distorted) to 23% in 1994 (or a rise of over 1,000%). By 1998, it would reach over 36%.[107] Income inequality also escalated, as measured by a Gini index, from 0.26 in 1991 to 0.41 in 1994. The fall in living standards was accompanied by a rise in the mortality rate of nearly 50% (which increased from 10.7 per 1,000 persons in 1988 to 15.7 in 1994). These trends were accompanied by diminishing life expectancy

---

[106] The European Commission broadly coordinates its actions in the CIS/Balkans regions with those of the World Bank, through a Memorandum of Understanding.

[107] An emblematic and haunting image of those days is the picture of pensioners being paid in kind (commonly in *bread*, which they would themselves have to sell in open stalls to acquire money). At that time, the state was unable to pay their pensions in cash (as the state itself was being paid in kind by taxpayers, in a chain of barter transactions).

(from 69.5 years in 1989 to 64.3 in 1994), with a consequent population reduction (from 148.3 million in 1990 to under 143 million in 2006).

The years of accumulated strong growth altered this picture greatly. By December 2007, unemployment in Russia had fallen to 6% (ILO methodology), halving its post-1998 level (see Figure 2.7). As a consequence of the prolonged economic boom, some regions of Russia effectively face labour shortages.

Figure 2.7 Unemployment and poverty

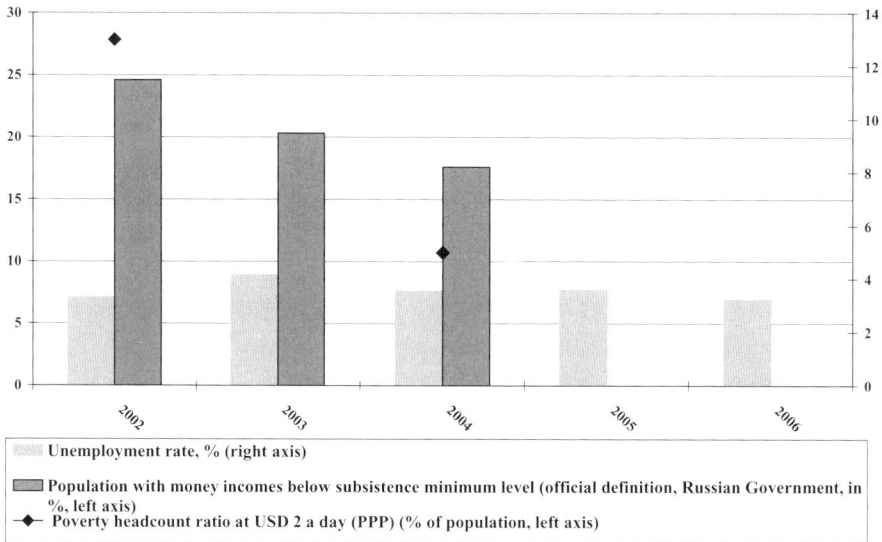

Unemployment rate, % (right axis)

Population with money incomes below subsistence minimum level (official definition, Russian Government, in %, left axis)
Poverty headcount ratio at USD 2 a day (PPP) (% of population, left axis)

Sources: Rosstat and WDI.

Also, following the CIS-wide trend of strong reductions in poverty and in income inequalities, the poverty rate in Russia fell from 36% in the aftermath of the 1998 financial crisis to 17% in 2004, with almost 20 million Russians being lifted out of poverty in the space of a few years. The share of households whose income was less than $2 a day had fallen to around 4% in 2004. There has been a small reduction in inequality, with the Gini index falling from its post-1998 high of 0.37 to 0.34 in 2002.[108] although it is

---

[108] As a comparator, the Gini index for Brazil, China and South Africa were respectively, 0.58 (2003), 0.45 (2001) and 0.58 (2000). Germany scored 0.28 (2000) in this index.

not clear if this reduction trend continued afterwards. A retrenchment in social expenditures is also being reversed. This is partially being done through the National Priority Projects for health, education, housing and agriculture, which are expected to add 0.8% of GDP in expenditures in those areas during 2007.

On the other hand, the Russian *official* population continues to age and shrink,[109] although life expectancy seems to have started to increase again, reaching 65.8 years in 2005, as has fertility. Mortality rates are still very high in Russia, particularly among working-age men. The rate of population increase in Russia is the world's second lowest: -0.6%, just above Ukraine's -0.8%. The UN forecasts a population decline in Russia during the period 2004–50 of 22% (from 144 to 112 million). In order to compensate this decline in full, an annual inflow of around *1 million* working-age migrants would be necessary. As there is no visa regime among the CIS countries (with the exception of Georgia), formal immigration flows have indeed been quite substantial, especially in the last few years. More specifically, the Russian Federal Migration Service issued 650,000 work permits to foreigners in 2005 alone, and it estimates that there may be up to *14 million – legal and illegal – foreign workers* in the country (or around 10% of the entire Russian population). According to census data, until 2002 most of the decline in the Russian population (5%) was compensated by a net migration of 3.8%. Given the very large volume of unregistered migration, it may even have fully compensated the population fall.

This large number of foreign workers is relatively recent, corresponding to the later stages of Russia's resumption of growth. With the aim of addressing this large and mostly unregulated migrant population, and after several ethnic and xenophobic incidents during 2006, Russia introduced a new migration law in late 2006. Under it, a quota of 6 million foreign workers was set for 2007. The new legislation also relaxes the rather stringent procedures for CIS and other foreign citizens to obtain legal work permits. At the same time, it increases fines for businesses that

---

[109] Russia's official resident population fell to 142.2 million in 2007, from 143.5 million in 2005.

employ illegal migrants. Additionally, a government decree restricts the number of non-Russians working in the retail trade.[110]

The strong increase Russia experienced in social inequality and exclusion in its post-transition period has been significantly reversed by the post-1998 growth. Still, as in so many domains, continued reform is necessary, especially in areas such as pensions (see Gurvich, 2007), health care and the regulation of migration.

---

[110] In late 2007, in the wake of the EU–Russia visa facilitation agreement, a reform of the visa procedures was introduced.

3. CONCLUSIONS: A DIFFERENT COUNTRY

This study has described the substantial changes observed in Russia since the end of the USSR. It has charted the wrenching initial period of massive economic and social dislocation following the collapse of the Soviet Union and the introduction of market economy institutions, to the apparent stabilisation of the mid-1990s and the subsequent crisis of 1998. It has also traced the resumption of growth, sustained from 1999 onwards, generated by the accumulated effects of economic and structural reforms and high energy prices. After the momentous changes of the past 15 years, synthetically captured by the data in Table 3.1, Russia can now truly be called a *different country*. The limited effects suffered so far by Russia from the wave of financial instability that began in August 2007 – a far cry from the 1998 crisis (while recognising the remaining structural fragilities of the Russian banking system) – also demonstrate how much the country has changed.

The discussion has shown that Russia's macro performance does not underperform that of other genuinely similar countries, either before or after 1998. The length and intensity of its transitional recession during the early to mid-1990s was related to the later start of reforms in the CIS countries, the depth of distortions accumulated by the three generations of a centrally planned economy and the lack of a binding external anchor, such as the EU accession process. The situation of the USSR was further aggravated by a national break-up. It is therefore incorrect to compare Russia's performance with the new EU member states: there are some similarities, but the differences are much more profound.

Table 3.1 Russia, before and after 1998

	1989–98 average	1999-2007 Average	2007
GDP (nominal $ billion)	221	579	1348
Growth (%)	-6.3	7.0	8.1
Inflation (%)	570	22.3	11.9
Budget balance (% GDP)	-10.5	3.3	5.6
Current account balance (% GDP)	1.6	10.3	6
Unemployment (%)	9.1	8.6	6.1

Sources: IMF and Rosstat.

The 1998 crisis was part of a string of similar crises throughout the 1990s, linked to the underlying unsustainability of a hard(er) exchange rate regime without a consistent policy mix in an environment of liberalised capital flows (admittedly coupled with some microeconomic vulnerabilities). The 1992–93 travails of the first exchange rate mechanism in the EU, the 1994 Mexican collapse, the 1997 Asian crisis, the 1999 Brazilian one and the 2001 Argentinian experience all generally fall into this category. Russia's post-1999 performance is rather impressive, especially when compared with similar economies (both commodity-exporting and non-commodity exporting ones), in terms of both GDP and inflation.

Even in terms of structural reform, when benchmarked against broadly similar economies (either other CIS countries or the other emerging giants of the BRICS), Russia's performance is respectable. All the fundamental structures of a market economy have been established – frequently at considerable social and economic cost – and the macroeconomic framework is clearly much more robust than it was in the mid-1990s. Additionally, despite the perception conveyed by some analyses, structural reform – albeit slower in certain areas – has not stopped.

That is not to say that a substantial, unfinished reform agenda does not remain: it does, and it includes some macro components, but mostly microeconomic and structural ones

In terms of the macro challenges, how to cope with the reduction and *eventual disappearance of the current account surplus* is likely to be the most important matter for medium-term policy. This change will imply a *need for continued positive net capital inflows*, and the only way to assure that is to create a *reliable investment climate*, itself a structural reform challenge. More investment and thus a better investment climate will equally be necessary for that perennial Russian problem, the need to diversify the economy away from the commodities sector.

These issues are linked to the *reform of the Russian state institutions and policies*. Here the credible available instrument is primarily the continued support for the reformist institutions within the Russian government but also for the wider apparatus of the Russian state and for the international *fora* that enable the sharing of international best practice with the Russian government. The full use of external anchors for reform, including the G8, WTO accession, OECD membership, the future EU–Russia framework agreement, the EU–Russia deep free trade agreement and the EU–Russia Sectoral Dialogues, is a feasible, necessary and important part of this strategy.

In the area of most immediate strategic relevance for the EU, the *energy industry*, continued reforms and the opening-up of the sector are necessary, especially now in an environment of rapidly increasing capital inflows into Russia. Reform in this area is thus tightly bound with the *reform of FDI legislation* in Russia. Negative developments, such as the continued domestic and external expansion of large state-owned enterprises in the energy sector, and the persistent uncertainty faced by foreign investors concerning the legal framework for FDI, are only partially mitigated by some positive steps, the most recent being the December 2006 timetable for the liberalisation of domestic energy prices. Given the strong interest of some of those state-owned enterprises in expanding their presence in EU markets, there may be a window of opportunity to achieve a greater liberalisation of the energy sector in Russia – a liberalisation that is primarily positive for Russia itself – for access to the unified EU energy market, but this can only be achieved if the EU acts in a consistent and effective way.

Nevertheless, in the end only the Russians themselves will be able to assure the consistent implementation of reforms. And this will only occur if a clear, coherent and convincing case is made demonstrating that such reforms will ultimately be beneficial, and mostly so for Russia and its population.

BIBLIOGRAPHY

Aghion, P. and E. Bessonova (2006), "On Entry and Growth: Theory and Evidence", *Revue de l'OFCE*, 2006/3.

Aghion, P. and O. Blanchard (1998), "On Privatization Methods in Eastern Europe and their Implications", *Economics of Transition*, Vol. 6, No. 1, pp. 87-99.

Ahrend, R. (2006), "Russia's Economic Expansion 1999–2005", in L. Vinhas de Souza and O. Havrylyshyn (eds), *Growth Resumption in the CIS*, Berlin: Springer Verlag.

Ahrend, R., D. de Rosa and W. Tompson (2006), *Does Russia Suffer from Dutch Disease? A Comparison of Russia's and Ukraine's Industrial Sectors*, OECD Economics Department Working Paper No. 540, OECD, Paris.

Appel, H. (1997), "Voucher Privatisation in Russia: Structural Consequences and Mass Response in the Second Period of Reform", *Europe-Asia Studies*, Vol. 49, No. 8, pp. 1433–49.

Arezki, R. and F. van der Ploeg (2007), *Can Natural Resource Course be Turned into a Blessing? The Role of Trade Policies and Institutions*, IMF Working Paper 07/55, International Monetary Fund, Washington, D.C.

Åslund, A. (2001), *The Myth of Output Collapse after Communism*, Working Paper No. 18, Carnegie Endowment for International Peace, Washington, D.C.

Beck, R., A. Kamps and E. Mileva (2007), "Long-Term Growth Prospects of the Russian Economy", mimeo, European Central Bank, Frankfurt.

Berg, A., E. Borenzstein, R. Sahay and J. Zettelmeyer (1999), *The Evolution of Output in Transition Economies: Explaining the Differences*, IMF Working Paper 99/73, International Monetary Fund, Washington, D.C.

Boussena, S. and C. Locatelli (2005), "The Bases of a New Organisation of the Russian Oil Sector: Between Private and State Ownership", mimeo.

Blaszczyk, B., I. Hoshi, E. Kocenda and R. Woodward (2003), "Ownership and Performance in Transition Economies: An Overview", in B. Blaszczyk, I. Hoshi and R. Woodward (eds.), *Secondary Privatisation in Transition Economies*, London: Palgrave, pp. 1-21.

Blustein, P. (2001), *The Chastening: Inside the Crisis that Rocked the Global Financial System and Humbled the IMF*, New York: PublicAffairs.

British Petroleum (BP) (2006), *Statistical Review of World Energy 2006*, BP Plc, London.

Campos, N. (2000), "Growth in Transition: What We Know, What We Don't Know and What We Should", mimeo.

Chiodo, A. and M. Owyang (2002), "A Case Study of a Currency Crisis: The Russian Default of 1998", *Review*, Federal Reserve Bank of Saint Louis, November/December 2002, pp. 7-17.

De Broek, M., and V. Koen (2000), *The Great Contractions in Russia, the Baltics and other FSU Countries: A View from the Supply Side*, IMF Working Paper 00/32, International Monetary Fund, Washington, D.C.

Deutsche Bank, *Russia Economics Monthly*, various issues.

Easterly, W. and S. Fisher (1994), *The Soviet Economic Decline: Historical and Republican Data*, Policy Research Working Paper No. 1284, World Bank, Washington, D.C.

Esanov, A., C. Merkl and L. Vinhas de Souza (2005), "Monetary Policy Rules for Russia", *Journal of Comparative Economics*, Vol. 33, No. 3, pp. 484–99.

European Bank for Reconstruction and Development (EBRD) (several issues), *Transition Report*, EBRD, London.

--------- (2007), *Law in Transition 2007*, EBRD, London.

European Commission (2007), *European Neighbourhood Policy: Economic Review of ENP Countries*, Occasional Paper No. 30, Directorate–General for Economic and Financial Affairs, Brussels.

--------- Moscow Delegation "E-Notes" (several reports).

Freinkman, L. and P. Yossifov (1998), "Decentralisation in Regional Fiscal Systems in Russia: Trend and Links to Economic Performance", mimeo, World Bank.

Guriev, S. and B. Ickes (2000), "Microeconomic Aspects of Economic Growth in Eastern Europe and the Former Soviet Union, 1950–2000", mimeo.

Gurvich, E. (2007), "The Prospects of the Russian Pension System", mimeo, Moscow.

Gylfason, T., T. Herbertson and G. Zoega (1997), *A Mixed Blessing: Natural Resources and Economic Growth*, Discussion Paper No. 1668, Centre for Economic and Policy Research, London.

Gylfason, T. (2000), *Resources, Agriculture, and Economic Growth in Economies in Transition*, CERGE-EI Working Paper No. 157, Center for Economic Research and Graduate Education - Economics Institute, Prague.

Habib, M. and M. Kalamova (2007), *Are there Oil Currencies? The Real Exchange Rate of Oil Exporting Countries*, ECB Working Paper No. 839, European Central Bank, Frankfurt.

Hanson, P. (2003), "The Russian Economic Recovery: Do Four Years of Growth tell us that the Fundamentals have Changed?", *Europe-Asia Studies*, Vol. 55, No. 3, pp. 365–82.

International Energy Agency (IEA) (2006a), *Energy Balances of Non-OECD Countries 2003–2004*, IEA, Paris.

––––––––– (2006b), *World Energy Outlook 2006*, IEA, Paris.

International Monetary Fund (IMF) (several years), *Article IV Consultations and Selected Issues for Russia*, IMF, Washington, D.C.

Kalyuzhnova, Y. (2005), "The EU and the Caspian Sea Region: An Energy Partnership?", *Economic Systems*, Vol. 29, No. 1, pp. 59–76.

Kotz, D. and F. Weir (2007), *Russia's Path from Gorbachev to Putin – The demise of the Soviet System and the New Russia*, London/New York: Routledge.

Kornai, J. (1994), "Transformational Recession: The Main Causes", *Journal of Comparative Economics*, Vol. 19, pp. 39–63.

Kozarzewski, P. and R. Woodward (2003), "Ownership and Performance of Firms Privatised by Management Employee Buyouts", in B. Blaszczyk, I. Hoshi and R. Woodward (eds.), *Secondary Privatisation in Transition Economies*, London: Palgrave, pp. 91–122.

Krueger, G. and M. Ciolko (1998), "A Note on Initial Conditions and Liberalisation during Transition", *Journal of Comparative Economics*, Vol. 26, pp. 718–34.

Kwon, G. (2003), "Post-crisis Fiscal Revenue Developments in Russia: From an Oil Perspective", *Public Finance and Management*, Vol. 3, No. 4, pp. 505–30.

Liuhto, K. (2007), *The Future Role of Foreign Firms in Russia's Strategic Industries*, Pan-European Institute 4/2007, Turku School of Economics.

Lysenko, T. and L. Vinhas de Souza (2007), *The Effects of Energy Price Shocks on Growth and Macroeconomic Stability in Selected Energy-Importing CIS Countries*, Occasional Paper No. 30, European Commission, Brussels, pp. 3–23.

Manzano, O. and R. Rigobon (2001) "Resource Curse or Debt Overhang?", NBER Working Paper No. 8390, National Bureau of Economic Research, Cambridge, MA.

Matsen, E. and R. Torvik (2005), "Optimal Dutch Disease", *Journal of Development Economics*, Vol. 78, No. 2, pp. 494–515.

Mau, V. and I. Starodubrovskaya (2001), *The Challenge of Revolution*, Oxford: Oxford University Press.

Merlevede, B., B. Van Aarle and K. Schoors (2004), *Russia from Bust to Boom: Oil, Politics or the Ruble?*, William Davidson Institute Working Paper No. 722, University of Michigan.

Ministry of Energy of the Russian Federation (2005), *Updated Draft Energy Strategy of the Russian Federation for the Period up to 2020*, Ministry of Energy of the Russian Federation Moscow.

Neville, P. (2003), *Russia: The USSR, the CIS and the Independent States*, London: Phoenix.

Odling-Smee, J. (2004), *The IMF and Russia in the 1990s*, IMF Working Paper 04/155, International Monetary Fund, Washington, D.C.

Organisation for Economic Cooperation and Development (OECD) (2006a), *OECD Investment Policy Review: Russian Federation*, OECD, Paris.

––––––––– (2006b), *OECD Economic Surveys: Russian Federation*, OECD, Paris.

––––––––– (2004), *OECD Economic Surveys: Russian Federation*, OECD, Paris.

Ofer, G. (1987), "Soviet Economic Growth: 1928-85", *Journal of Economic Literature*, Vol. XXV, pp. 1767–1833.

Ollus, S. and S. Barisitz (2007), *The Russian Non-Fuel Sector: Signs of Dutch Disease? Evidence from EU-25 Import Competition*, BOFIT Working Paper No. 2007/2, Bank of Finland Institute for Economies in Transition, Helsinki.

Oomes, N. and K. Kalcheva (2007), *Diagnosing Dutch Disease: Does Russia have the Symptoms?*, BOFIT Working Paper No. 2007/7, Bank of Finland Institute for Economies in Transition, Helsinki.

Owen, D. and D. Robinson (eds) (2003), *Russia Rebounds*, International Monetary Fund, Washington, D.C.

Roland, G. and T. Verdier (1999), "Transition and the Output Fall", *Economics of Transition*, Vol. 7, No. 1, pp. 1–28.

Rosefielde, S. (2005), "Russia: An Abnormal Country", *European Journal of Comparative Economics*, Vol. 2, No. 1, pp. 3–16.

"Russian Oil and Gas" (2005), *Australian Commodities*, Vol. 12, No. 2, pp. 361–78.

Sachs, J. and M. Warner (1995), *Natural Resource Abundance and Economic Growth*, NBER Working Paper No. 5398, National Bureau of Economic Research, Cambridge, MA.

Sapir, J. (2003), "Russia's Economic Growth and European Integration", *Post-Soviet Affairs*, Vol. 19, No. 1, January, pp. 1–23,

Shleifer, A. and D. Treisman (2005), "A Normal Country: Russia after Communism", *Journal of Economic Perspectives*, Vol. 19, No. 1, pp. 151–74.

Simola, H. (2007), *Russia Getting Closer to WTO Membership – What are the Practical Implications?*, BOFIT Working Paper No. 2007/3, Bank of Finland Institute for Economies in Transition, Helsinki..

Tompson, W. (2004), *Restructuring Russia's Electricity Sector: Towards Effective Competition or Faux Liberalisation?*, OECD Economics Department Working Paper No. 403, OECD, Paris.

Troika Dialog, *Russia Economics Monthly* (various issues).

United Nations Conference on Trade and Development (UNCTAD) (2007a), *World Investment Report 2007*, United Nations, New York and Geneva.

––––––––– (2007b), *World Investment Prospects Survey 2007–2009*, United Nations, New York and Geneva.

––––––––– (2006), *World Investment Report 2006*, United Nations, New York and Geneva.

Vercueil, J. (2007), "Russia and the WTO: On the Finishing Stretch", *Russie.Nei.Visions*, No. 16, Institut français des relations intenationales Russia/NIS Centre.

Vinhas de Souza, L. (2008), "Foreign Investment in Russia", *Country Focus Series*, European Commission, Directorate–General for Economic and Financial Affairs, Vol. 5, No. 1.

--------- (2006), "The Bank Lending Channel in the Russian Federation: An Initial Estimation", *Credit and Banking*, 9/2006, pp. 3–13.

--------- (2004a), *Financial Liberalisation and Business Cycles: The Experience of the New EU Member States in The Baltics and Central Eastern Europe*, Working Paper Series No. 22/04, Deutsche Bundesbank, Frankfurt.

--------- (2004b), "Financial Sector Development in the Future EU Member States and Russia", mimeo.

--------- (2003), *Beyond Transition: Essays on the Monetary Integration of the Accession Countries in Eastern Europe*, Amsterdam: Rozenberg, Thela Thesis.

Vinhas de Souza, L. and O. Havrylyshyn (2006), *Growth Resumption in the CIS*, Berlin: Springer Verlag.

World Bank (2007), *Doing Business 2008*, World Bank, Washington, D.C.

--------- (2006), *Russian Economic Report No. 12*, World, Bank, Moscow.

--------- (2004), *Russia: Transition Meets Development, Country Economic Memorandum for the Russian Federation*, World Bank, Moscow.

--------- (2003), *Russian Economic Report No. 6*, World Bank, Moscow.

--------- (2000), "Privatisation Revenue Trends in the Region 1990-1998", *Global Development Finance 2000*, World Bank, Washington, D.C.

World Economic Forum (WEF) (2007), *Global Competitiveness Report 2007*, WEF, Geneva.